# LIVING WITNESSES

# LIVING WITNESSES

## BY SCOTT WEIDENSAUL

THE
APPLE
PRESS

**A QUINTET BOOK**

Published by The Apple Press
6 Blundell Street
London N7 9BH

ISBN 1-85076-394-1

This book was designed and produced by
Quintet Publishing Limited
6 Blundell Street
London N7 9BH

Creative Director: Richard Dewing
Designers: Ian Hunt, Stuart Walden
Project Editor: William Hemsley
Editor: Steven Luck

Typeset in Great Britain by
Central Southern Typesetters, Eastbourne
Manufactured in Singapore by
Bright Arts (S) Pte Ltd
Printed in Hong Kong by
Leefung-Asco Printers Limited

# CONTENTS

# INTRODUCTION

T here are, by possibly conservative estimates, somewhere between 10 and 50 million living species on Earth, ranging from plants to tiny microbes to the great whales. Life's diversity is breathtaking; a single hectare of rain forest may hold 300 species of tree, thousands of types of smaller plants, hundreds of species of butterfly, countless forms of beetle, and much more.

Yet as striking as life today may be, it is only the latest chapter in a story nearly 3 thousand million years old. Today's familiar animals – lions and giraffes, trout and parrots, house cats and barnyard pigs – are the result of unexpected twists and turns of evolution, the descendants of extinct animals that to our eyes were bizarre, sometimes frightening, but always fascinating.

**BELOW: Earth sustains an astonishing diversity of life; a single hectare of rain forest may hold as many as 300 kinds of trees and a myriad of other plants and animals: butterflies, macaws, frogs and caimans among them.**

# HOW EVOLUTION WORKS

People have known for hundreds of years that animals can change; any farmer selectively breeding cows, or fish fancier cross-breeding strains of guppies, can see that it happens. Recognition that the "dragon bones" of the Far East and fossil reptiles of Europe were not the remains of mythical creatures, or casualties of Noah's Flood, came in the late 18th and early 19th centuries, but even after scientists realized that organisms changed drastically over the course of time, they were unclear about how such changes could occur in nature.

The first theory that provided a successful explanation was proposed by Charles Darwin (Alfred Russell Wallace developed the same ideas independently at about the same time, but did not develop his ideas as far). Darwin's theory first appeared in full in *The Origin of Species* (1859), and stated that evolution proceeded by a process of natural selection. The theory, with some modification (especially to take account of developments in the study of genetics), is still held by the great majority of biologists.

What Darwin argued was that, even within the same species, individuals differ from one another in ways that may be slight but can be significant. If one of these differences aids an individual in its struggle to survive, the individual tends to have more offspring than do other individuals. Many of the offspring inherit the advantageous characteristic, and in turn have a larger number of offspring. In this way, the proportion of individuals in the population that have the characteristic increases until the feature is in all animals of the species.

Individuals in a population vary, and occasionally advantageous mutations occur that add yet more useful variety. The changes in the characteristics of a population of organisms may be very slow, but there are many millions of years over which they can occur.

**BELOW: The blue-footed booby of the Galapagos islands was one of the unusual animals that inspired Darwin to his theories of natural selection.**

**ABOVE: Organisms change over the course of time because those with better adaptations to their environments are more likely to survive and reproduce – what Darwin referred to as natural selection, or "survival of the fittest".**

# THE CALENDAR OF LIFE

It is difficult even for specialists to comprehend the staggering time scale involved in any discussion of prehistory. Our lives are very short in contrast, and to grasp lengths of time that may be tens of millions of times longer is almost impossible.

To make such enormous scales of time more comprehensible, scientists have divided time into a hierarchy (see page 58). The largest divisions are the *eons,* each of which is divided into *eras* and then *periods.* Many divisions have tongue-twisting names such as Ordovician and Quaternary. The more recent periods are divided further still into *epochs.* This hierarchy of time is called the geological timescale and is essential to any understanding of the history of life. Because they often begin and end with mass extinctions, the divisions of time are not equal in length: the Triassic period, for example, lasted about 35 million years, while the Jurassic, which followed it immediately, lasted 69 million years, and the next, the Cretaceous, 79 million.

Even with the geologic calendar, immensities of time are hard to grasp. One common technique for converting the history of Earth into a manageable form is to, quite literally, set it to a calendar, with January 1 representing the formation of the planet. On that scale, bacteria did not evolve until June 30, multicellular life did not appear until late summer, and the first vertebrates around November 20. Humans are among the latest of all; we did not rise to our hind legs until New Year's Eve.

**ABOVE: Once considered "dragon bones" or the remnants of the biblical Flood, fossils were first recognized as the remains of extinct, ancient creatures in the 17th century.**

**BELOW: Knowing the hierarchical divisions of time created by geologists is important for putting evolution into perspective (see page 58). Lizards, for example, first appear in the fossil record during the Triassic period.**

# WHERE IS LIFE GOING?

## TANYSTROPHEUS

*An animal such as a Tanystropheus seems to have evolved such an extreme characteristic in its long neck that it is hard to imagine it surviving. Yet the neck was, no doubt, an efficient hunting mechanism, probably used in darting after quick-moving fish. Indeed, through the evolution of the several species of Tanystropheus, neck length tended to increase, indicating that a extremely long neck was a useful survival aid.*

We often think of extinct organisms as somehow inferior to those surviving today. It makes sense: if they had not been, they would not have died out. This simply is not true, however. Evolution does not march inexorably from the less perfect to the more perfect, nor were extinct species obsolete when compared to modern relatives. At each step of the way, the living forms of the day were suited to their environment. Today, those that retain ancient forms, or are unspecialized when compared to their relatives, are often referred to as "primitive" – but this should not be taken as a judgment.

The opossum, for example, is often called a primitive mammal. It is a marsupial, for one thing, giving birth to tiny, poorly formed young that must undergo a prolonged period of development in the mother's pouch; the young of placental mammals, on the other hand, undergo much of their development in the mother's womb. Opossum fossils, remains of animals little different from today's species, date as far back as the Age of Dinosaurs.

But the fact that an animal has not changed does not mean it is imperfect – in fact, one could argue the opposite. Opossums have remained much the same because they are so well adapted to a thoroughly modern environment. Indeed, the Virginia opossum has greatly expanded its range in the past 200 years, so that it is now found over much of North America – something many more "modern" mammals have proved unable to achieve.

Neither are the living species that share our world a logical end-product of evolution. It is easy to look back on the history of life – invertebrate to vertebrate, fish to amphibian to reptile to mammal – and assume smugly that such a process would naturally result in sentient beings like ourselves. Once again, this is not true. For one thing, natural selection pushes life in many directions. Evolution is not a tidy line but a tangled, overlapping bush with countless branches. We are also coming to realize that the history of life involves a long tale of catastrophes, in which almost unimaginable disasters have wiped out almost all life on many occasions.

It apparently mattered little how well-suited an organism was to its environment; during mass extinctions many previously successful groups vanished, their place taken by others that had been relegated to a minor role before. The evolutionary bush is pruned periodically – and without such prunings, who knows how life would have evolved. For example, consider that about 165 million years ago, both the mammals and the reptiles that would become the dinosaurs first appeared. The mammals stayed small and insignificant, but the dinosaurs went on to produce one of the greatest flowerings of vertebrate evolution in history. They inhabited and thrived in all the major environmental niches for more than 100 million years, until they finally disappeared at the end of the Cretaceous. There is a growing body of evidence that an extraterrestrial impact – an asteroid, meteor or comet – was responsible for this particular mass extinction. Only with the extinction of the dinosaurs were the mammals able to diversify and capture the niches previously held by the giant reptiles.

What we think of as mammalian dominance today is not the result of better genes or inexorable progress – it was probably, quite simply, just good luck.

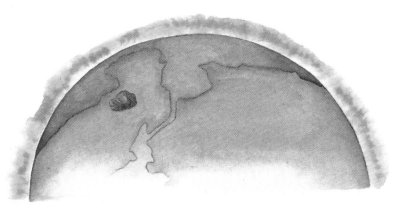

**ABOVE AND RIGHT: The theory that a meteorite caused the extinction of the dinosaurs states that when the meteorite in question struck the Earth's surface it threw a large amount of debris into the air. This debris was dispersed in a cloud through the atmosphere. The cloud caused many months or even years of darkness resulting in considerable disruption of global eco-systems and perhaps the demise of the dinosaurs.**

**BELOW: If a large meteorite striking the Earth caused climatic changes – such as a sudden drop in temperature – this would probably not have directly killed the dinosaurs. The greatest problems for these creatures would probably have arisen from disruption of food chains and other such ecological changes.**

# FISH

We human beings are chordates – that is, we possess a long bundle of spinal nerves encased in a stiff, hardened spinal column, the backbone. This feature marks every vertebrate, from 150-ton (tonne) blue whales to bee hummingbirds that weigh less than a penny.

The most primitive chordates were always thought to be similar to the lancelets – jawless, eel-like creatures with a notochord, the simplistic forerunner of the backbone. Now, however, a re-examination of the detailed Burgess Shale fossils from Canada – fossils dating back more than 530 million years, to the Cambrian period – has shown that what was once thought a worm is actually the first known chordate. Named *Pikaia*, it was small and looked rather like a leech, but it, too, had the notochord and muscular structure of later vertebrates.

Chordate evolution was strictly an aquatic affair for several hundred million years. The first fish were agnathans, jawless like today's lampreys, which over the course of time grew steadily more complex and armoured – the latter providing protection from scorpion-like eurypterids, some more than 8 feet/2.4 metres long and by far the most dangerous predator of the time. These were still primitive fish by our standards, however. Known as ostracoderms, or "shell-skins", these fish of the Silurian period had no jaw bones (just a fleshy mouth), no paired fins, and probably only the most rudimentary swimming ability when compared to modern fish.

The Silurian also saw the first appearance of jaws, which were probably the result of modified gill arches for supporting the mouth. Jaws (and teeth) gave their owners access to a wider range of food than their jawless predecessors, and opened new avenues for fish evolution. The Devonian period saw an explosion of fish, among them the 30-foot/9-metre predator *Dinichthys*, which had an armoured head and sharp, beaked mouth.

The Devonian also brought a great split in fish evolution, with one group – represented today by sharks, skates and rays – possessing skeletons of cartilage. The other, and ultimately much more successful, group was the bony fishes, which today number in the many thousands of species.

## ANCIENT FISHES

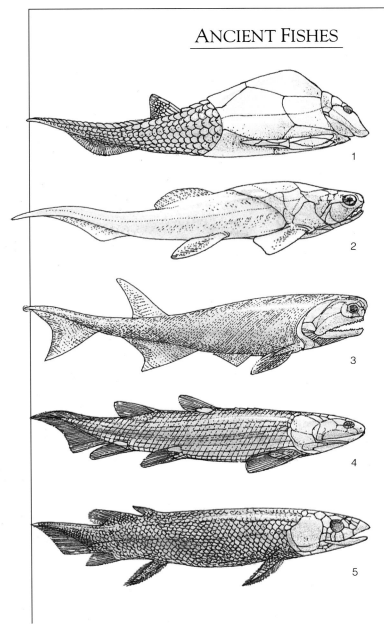

*Five fishes, the fossilized remains of which were found in the Old Red Sandstone in Scotland, all showing some degree of armour on the front parts of their bodies. The first two, Pterichthyodes (1) and Coccosteus (2), belong to an entirely extinct group. Cheirolepsis (3) is a bony fish not unlike some modern forms. Osteolepsis (4) and Dipterus (5) belong to the lobe-finned group, close to the origin of the amphibians (see pages 18–23).*

**ABOVE: Paleontologists suspect that true jaws first arose in fish when a pair of bony gill supports migrated forward to provide a base for the mouth, which until then was just a fleshy hole.**

# SHARKS

Sharks are often placed near the bottom of fish family trees as "primitive" on account of their cartilaginous skeleton and early evolution. But if a body plan works there is no reason to change, and sharks have been successful with theirs for a very long time.

There are several hundred species of sharks around the world, ranging from deep-water varieties less than a foot/30 centimetres long to species as big as whales. Many sharks are bottom-dwellers or sluggish swimmers, like the horn and swell sharks. Others are streamlined inhabitants of open water, like the requiem and mackerel shark families, which include many

of the best-known and most fearsome shark species.

The ultimate expression of the predatory shark lifestyle may well be the great white shark, which exceeds 20 or 25 feet/6 or 7.5 metres in length. Robust and fast, great whites will eat almost anything, including humans, but no shark species considers people a natural source of food. In some regions great whites, for example, feed heavily on marine mammals like seals and sea lions; marine biologists believe many attacks on humans may be cases of mistaken identity.

Big as it is, the great white is by no means the largest shark in the world – that honour belongs to the whale shark, an utterly

inoffensive fish of up to 60 feet/18 metres in length that feeds on plankton. Although not as large, the basking shark, another filter feeder found in northern waters, can exceed a length of 45 feet/13.5 metres.

One must suppress a shudder at the thought of a shark as big as a basking shark and with the teeth and (presumably) hunting abilities of a great white, but such a creature did exist. This monster was *Carcharodon megalodon*, a great white ancestor that lived about 4 million years ago, and one of its triangular teeth covers a human hand. Previous reconstructions of *C. megalodon* showed a fish of between 60 and 90 feet/18 and 27 metres. Recent studies suggest it was only 40 feet/12 metres long, but it must have been an awesome hunter.

While *Carcharodon* teeth are relatively rare, the teeth of *Odontaspis* sand sharks are amazingly common along some sea coasts, where the action of waves and sand polishes the curved teeth and erodes away the triangular bases. Although the fossils are mainly from the Pliocene, sand sharks remain among the most common species in many coastal waters.

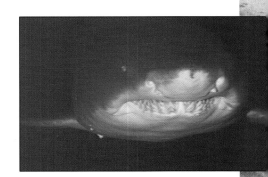

**RIGHT: The sand tiger shark is common in many temperate coastal waters around the world, and its teeth are abundant as Pleistocene fossils along a number of beaches in the United States.**

**BELOW: Sleek and beautiful, a blue shark slides effortlessly through the water, streamlined for a life in constant motion in the open sea.**

# THE COELACANTH: A GLIMPSE BACKWARDS

For biologists, the deep, black waters off the Comoros Islands, between Africa and Madagascar, are a little bit like a time machine. From their depths, on rare occasions, fishermen pull up a creature evocative of the bridge between sea and land, more than 370 million years ago. It is the coelacanth, the strange fish more properly known as *Latimeria*. Chunkily built, with a wide, tooth-studded mouth and a paddle-shaped tail with only a fringe of fin, the coelacanth is one of the lobefins, a group of fish that are found in fossils that date from as far back as the Devonian.

Paleontologists (scientists that study fossils) have always been keenly interested in lobefins, since this group (known as crossopterygians) are considered pivotal in the transition from fish to amphibians – a change covered in more detail in the next chapter. Fossil coelacanths are found in rock strata only until the Cretaceous, and there was never any reason to believe that they had not become extinct nearly 70 million years ago. No reason, that is, until 1938. In that year, a trawler working the waters off South Africa brought up a bizarre fish in its nets. It was so unlike anything else the crew – or the curator of a small museum on shore – had seen that experts were called in. To their amazement, the catch was found to be a coelacanth.

The scientific world was astonished, it was as though a dinosaur had been captured; indeed, *Latimeria* is usually called a living fossil, although it differs in several details from fossil lobefins, and represents a modern genus and species of that group. Despite many searches, 14 years went by before a second coelacanth was caught, this time in the Comoros – where, it turned out, the local fishermen had long been aware of the odd fish, which they caught by angling in water as deep as 1,300 feet/395 metres.

Since then, a number of coelacanths have been brought to shore, a few still living. The paired pectoral (chest) and pelvic (belly) fins, which in the descendants of ancient lobefins became legs, are held down and out at a 45-degree angle when the coelacanth swims, perhaps allowing the fish to scramble on the deep sea bottom. Or perhaps not; just because some lobefins modified their fins into legs doesn't mean they all used them that way, and *Latimeria*'s fins also seem to work well for their original purpose – swimming.

**BELOW:** *Latimeria,* **more commonly known as the coelacanth, is a lobefin. The lobefins are a group of fish at one time thought to have been extinct for 70 million years. The fish, indeed, seems ancient in appearance, and it is commonly referred to as a "living fossil".**

# BONY FISHES

There are only a few hundred species of cartilaginous fish in the world, but nearly 20,000 kinds of bony fish, from gobies as thin as a pencil lead to giant bluefin tuna, from electric eels capable of generating terrific shocks to the splendidly arrayed reef fish of the tropics.

The bony fish have conquered virtually every aquatic environment on Earth since their appearance in the Devonian. They live in hot springs in the desert, in Arctic lakes that freeze almost solid and in the abyssal depths where they must manufacture their own light with bioluminescent organs. Some, like the lungfish, have even evolved the ability to breathe air.

The salmonids – salmon, trout, whitefish and grayling – are typical bony fishes, and while from an evolutionary standpoint they are somewhat primitive in form, to many people, anglers in particular, they represent the height of fish development.

Salmonids are found throughout the Northern Hemisphere; the Atlantic salmon, for instance, inhabits both Europe and eastern North America, while the famous brown trout (now stocked in almost every continent) is a native of Europe.

The most unusual members of the family, however, are the Pacific slope salmon, including the chinook, coho, sockeye and chum salmon. They are anadromous, breeding in freshwater but maturing at sea, and their spawning runs are the stuff of legend; one race of chinook salmon travels for more than 1,000 miles/1,600 kilometres upriver before finally reaching its home streams.

Once in freshwater, the salmon undergo massive physical changes. The digestive tract shrinks, making room for egg or

**ABOVE: Kokanee, the landlocked form of the sockeye salmon, gather in their breeding colours at the mouth of a feeder stream.**

**BELOW: A pair of big chinook salmon battle a powerful current as they make their way upstream to spawn, a journey that may encompass hundreds of miles.**

sperm sacs; the males may develop viciously hooked jaws and humped backs; some species turn brilliant scarlet. Once in their spawning waters, the salmon pair and mate, racing the clock – for they are dying piece by piece, literally falling to shreds while they complete their last act of life. Eagles, bears and gulls come to feast on the wreckage. Only a single species of Pacific salmon, the steelhead, does not die at spawning, perhaps one reason why it was long classified as a variety of rainbow trout.

# AMPHIBIANS

# FROM WATER TO LAND

I t seems likely that the earliest amphibian-like fish moved onto land because it was a food-rich habitat empty of any vertebrates, not because their home pools were drying up – and not, as cartoonists like to portray the event, because it was the next step in some inevitable "march of progress".

One modern fish that has taken to a partially terrestrial life, the mudskipper of the tropics, inhabits tidal flats that for half the time are exposed to air – flats, in other words, that are beyond the reach of all other fish. By exploiting a new ecological niche, the mudskipper avoids competing with other fish. Thus, although they are not closely related to the amphibian ancestors, mudskippers show the advantages of moving onto land – advantages that would have been even more compelling millions of years ago.

Paleontologists date the transition from fish to amphibian as occurring in the mid- to late Devonian, when lobefin fish such as *Eusthenopteron* lived in shallow bodies of fresh water. *Eusthenopteron* had robust pectoral and pelvic fins, and while it could not have rotated them forward far enough to act as legs, they would have provided some degree of support whenever the fish wriggled onto land.

At around the same period, the oldest known amphibians, which at one time shared the rudimentary limb bones of the lobefins, evolved stronger, more elongated limbs, while

ABOVE: Urodeles, like this northern red salamander from the eastern parts of North America, are similar in shape to the earliest true amphibians to roam the Earth, which like the salamanders had short legs and long tails.

retaining the long body and skull pattern of the fish. They would have looked very much like the modern salamanders, the most primitive of the surviving amphibians.

The Carboniferous and early Permian periods were the heyday of the amphibians, before the ascendancy of the reptiles eclipsed them. Among the largest was *Eryops*, nearly 8 feet/2.4 metres long, and obviously a hunter of distinction –

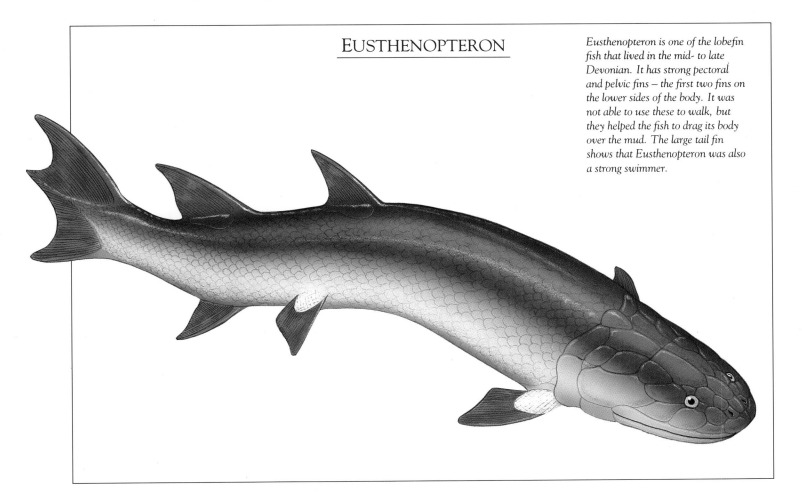

## EUSTHENOPTERON

*Eusthenopteron is one of the lobefin fish that lived in the mid- to late Devonian. It has strong pectoral and pelvic fins – the first two fins on the lower sides of the body. It was not able to use these to walk, but they helped the fish to drag its body over the mud. The large tail fin shows that Eusthenopteron was also a strong swimmer.*

although it, in turn, may well have been hunted by even larger early reptiles like the finbacked *Dimetrodon*.

Another Permian amphibian of note was *Diplocaulus*, an aquatic species with a bizarrely boomerang-shaped head. No one is quite sure why *Diplocaulus* needed the wide-flaring lobes; one theory holds that they were used for smashing rivals during courtship fights, while another contends the head shape would have acted like a wing in moving currents of water, permitting *Diplocaulus* to lunge quickly upwards at prey.

Although modern salamanders look much like their ancient ancestors, they have adapted. They are, for the most part, small terrestrial amphibians just a few inches long, with long tails and short legs; they have a sprawling posture with the belly dragging, and move with a series of wriggling, side-to-side

swings of the body that resemble the undulations of a swimming fish. This is the same low-hung position the earliest amphibians would have assumed as well.

As a group, salamanders and newts (those that live in water) are known as urodeles, and they are common in northern temperate zones around the world; for some reason, they are not nearly as common in the tropics, where the frogs and toads have been spectacularly successful. Instead, some of the greatest diversity of salamanders is found in the Appalachian ridges of eastern North America, where damp, cool peaks are separated by drier valleys that came into being as the climate warmed after the last ice age. Effectively cut off from others of their species, each isolated population evolved in different directions, producing a kaleidoscope of varieties.

Even though many salamanders live on land, they must stay in damp environments like wet leaves, or beneath rotting logs. Their eggs, too, must be laid where they will not dry out, since they are covered only by a thin layer of "jelly" that provides no protection against desiccation (drying out). Many species, like the spotted salamander, spend most of the year on dry land, but return each spring to woodland pools where they mate and lay their egg masses – only to then abandon them, for most amphibians provide no parental care.

**LEFT: Amphibians of the Carboniferous. In the foreground are two microsaurs, a highly terrestrial group, about 12 in/30 cm long. The *Dendrerpeton* is a much larger (about 8 ft/2.5 m) aquatic amphibian.**

**ABOVE: Many species of newts go through four stages – egg, gilled larva, terrestrial "eft" and aquatic adult. This is the eft stage of the red-spotted newt, the most common North American species.**

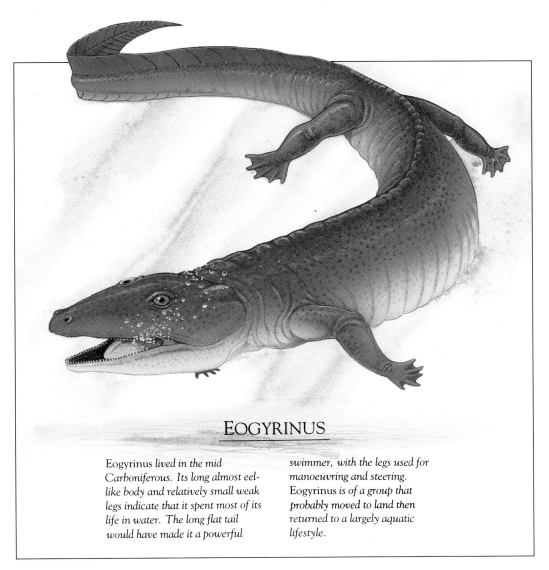

## EOGYRINUS

Eogyrinus *lived in the mid Carboniferous. Its long almost eel-like body and relatively small weak legs indicate that it spent most of its life in water. The long flat tail would have made it a powerful swimmer, with the legs used for manoeuvring and steering.* Eogyrinus *is of a group that probably moved to land then returned to a largely aquatic lifestyle.*

**BELOW: All amphibian larvae go through a gilled larval stage, although some do so in the egg. This is the large larva of the tiger salamander, which in some areas remain gilled all their lives.**

# VERTEBRATES FIND A VOICE

On a warm, drizzly night in spring, wade carefully into a shallow marsh almost anywhere in the world. Chances are your ears will be assaulted by a symphony of wild sound – creaks, peeps, chirps, croaks, groans, snores, trills and many more calls, all the products of amphibians.

The earliest Devonian amphibians were almost certainly silent; they lacked the notch in the skull to house an eardrum, and could not have heard airborne sound. But during the Carboniferous period, eared amphibians appeared, and amphibian reproduction has not sounded the same since.

Today, the frogs and toads – known as anurans, literally "without tails" – make best use of the amphibian voice. The tiny spring peeper, a treefrog no bigger than a fingernail, can produce a shrill peep that can be heard half-a-mile away; a pond crammed with thousands of them can be deafening. Each species has its own unique call. The calls are used to find a mate, hold a territory and drive away rivals – activities which salamanders accomplish through touch, posture and display.

Worldwide we know of more than 3,700 species of anurans, with more being discovered each year in the tropics; Peru alone, for example, has more than 800 species of treefrogs. Generally speaking, frogs have smooth, wet skin and are powerful jumpers, while toads have warty skin and tend to hop rather than leap.

Anurans first appear in the fossil record during the amphibian dispersion of the Carboniferous. Despite this early arrival, they are highly specialized animals; the backbone is considerably shortened, the hind legs and toes enlarged and the shoulder joints reinforced to cushion landings. The skull is wide and flat, with space for a large external eardrum – the round patch behind a frog's eye.

Being amphibians, modern anurans are still dependent on water, especially for reproduction, but they have evolved some ingenious ways around that limitation. In the treetop canopy of the rain forest, some frogs lay their eggs in the pools trapped by cup-shaped leaves; others create a mass of moisture-retaining froth on land into which the eggs are laid, and still others lay them underneath wet leaves.

A few anurans have even adapted to life in deserts, perhaps the least likely environment for an amphibian. The spadefoot toads of the southwestern area of the United States, as well as water-holding frogs of Australia and others, spend most of their time underground, waiting for the periodic downpours that hit all the driest deserts. With the rush of water they dig back to the surface and mate. The pools in which they lay their eggs dry quickly, so the tadpoles develop at a frantic pace. Often it is not fast enough, and the young die, but the plan succeeds sufficiently to ensure the species' survival.

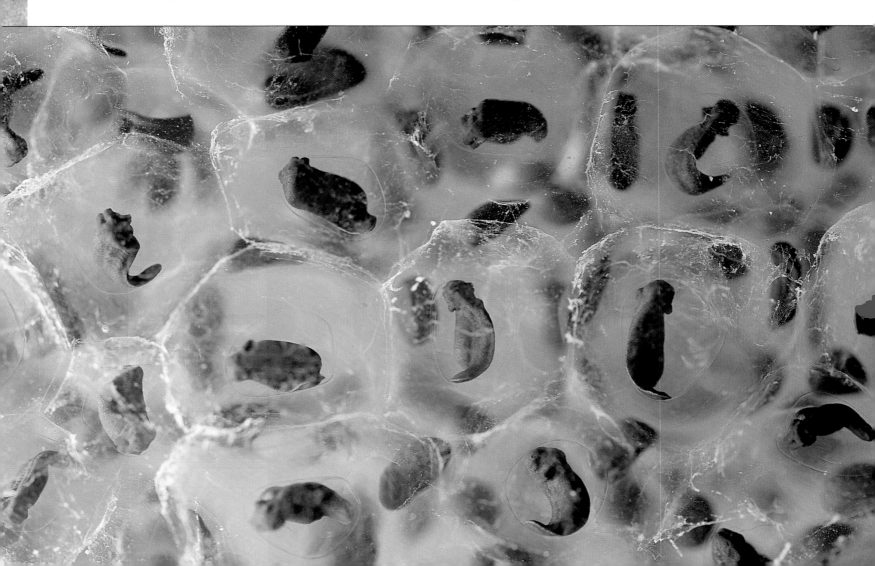

ABOVE AND RIGHT: With more than 3,700 species worldwide, anurans are the most diverse amphibians. Shown here is a tropical treefrog and a Peruvian leaf frog.

LEFT: Covered only by a gelatinous coat that does not prevent dehydration, amphibian eggs must be laid in water or a damp environment. These, laid by a wood frog, show the rapid development of the embryos in just two days.

# REPTILES

# THE EVOLUTION OF REPTILES

Many of the amphibians that evolved during the late Devonian, and which blossomed in the Carboniferous period, were terrestrial animals with one very important limitation – they still required water, many of them for their day-to-day lives, and all of them for breeding.

An amphibian egg contains the fertilized cell itself, surrounded by a gelatinous coating that provides some protection against fungal attack, but none at all against dehydration. For this reason, an amphibian must lay its eggs either in water or in a very damp environment, such as a moist burrow (in the case of many salamanders) or in a frothy bubble nest on land, as with some tropical treefrogs.

This dependence on water means that many places on Earth cannot be colonized by amphibians. However, the development of a new type of egg in the Devonian period overcame this problem. Known as an amniotic egg, it has a tough, water-resistant covering that prevents the egg from drying out. This development opened huge new vistas for the group in which it evolved, the amniotes.

The earliest amniotes so far found date from the Carboniferous and include a small creature known as *Hylonomus*, which may well have been the first true reptile. Today, reptiles are easily distinguished from amphibians by their scaly, watertight skin and shelled eggs, but neither eggs nor skin routinely fossilize, so paleontologists sometimes have difficulty deducing, from skeletal remains, just where to draw the line between the earliest amphibians and reptiles.

By the close of the Carboniferous, the amniotes split into three branches: anapsids, the most primitive of the group; the synapsids, which led to mammals; and diapsids, the evolution of which is believed to have led at length to turtles, lizards, snakes, crocodilians, dinosaurs and birds.

**LEFT:** *Hylonomus,* shown here against a background of Carboniferous forest, is one of the oldest known reptiles. The similarity in appearance to Carboniferous amphibians is clear, although the skin is one of the significant differences.

**OVERLEAF: Reptiles of the late Triassic in southern Brazil, a fauna that was typical of most of the world. The herbivores shown are the rhynchosaurs *Scaphonyx* (mid-left), the cynodont (see page 53), *Traversodon* (bottom left) and the dicynodont *Dinodeontosaurus* (deceased, right). The carnivores are *Rauisuchus* (top left), the cynodonts *Belesodon* (bottom right) and the archosaur *Staurikosaurus* (top left), which is possibly the oldest known dinosaur in the world.**

Staurikosaurus

Rauisuchus

Scaphonyx

Dinodontsaurus

Traversodon

Belesodon

# THE EVOLUTION OF THE REPTILE LIMB

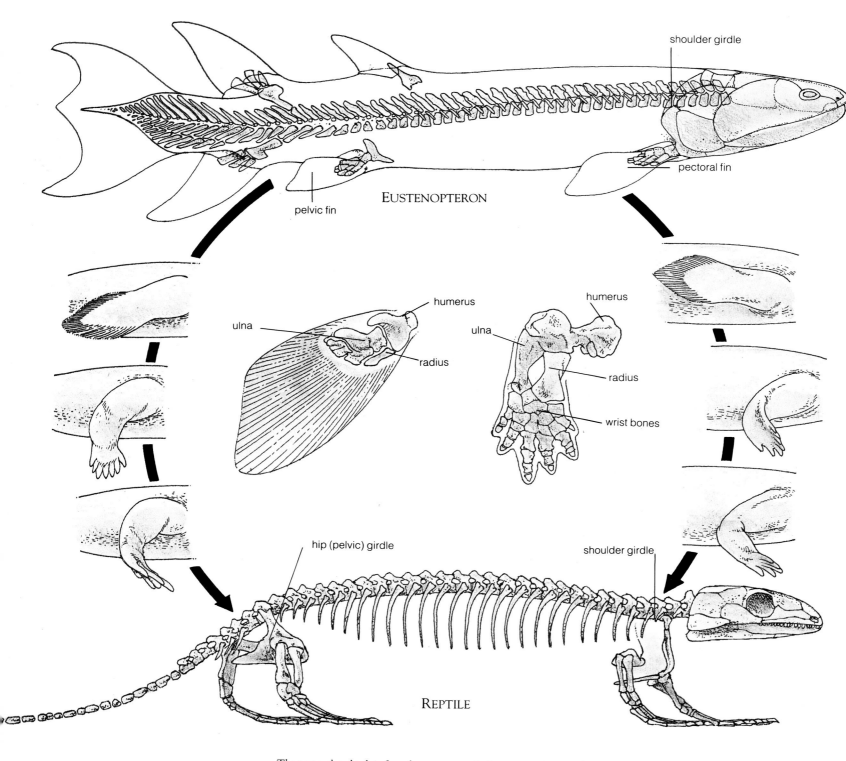

shoulder girdle

pectoral fin

EUSTENOPTERON

pelvic fin

humerus

ulna

radius

humerus

ulna

radius

wrist bones

hip (pelvic) girdle

shoulder girdle

REPTILE

The pectoral and pelvic fins of Eusthenopteron *look very different from the slender limbs of the typcial middle Carboniferous reptile, but many of the intermediate stages in this possible* evolutionary transition are known. Eusthenopteron *could certainly have moved its lobed fins backwards and forwards beneath the body; and the bones of the limbs of early amphibians show close resemblances.*

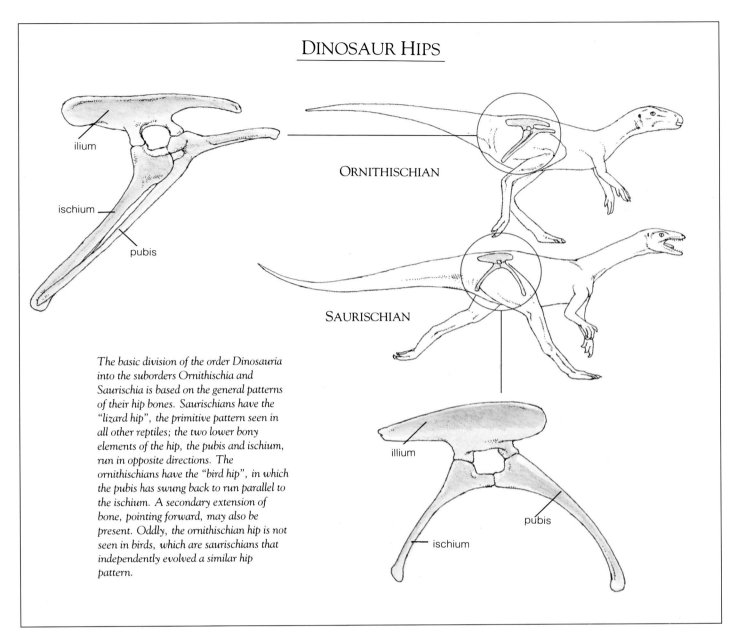

# DINOSAUR HIPS

ilium

ischium

pubis

ORNITHISCHIAN

SAURISCHIAN

illium

pubis

ischium

*The basic division of the order Dinosauria into the suborders Ornithischia and Saurischia is based on the general patterns of their hip bones. Saurischians have the "lizard hip", the primitive pattern seen in all other reptiles; the two lower bony elements of the hip, the pubis and ischium, run in opposite directions. The ornithischians have the "bird hip", in which the pubis has swung back to run parallel to the ischium. A secondary extension of bone, pointing forward, may also be present. Oddly, the ornithischian hip is not seen in birds, which are saurischians that independently evolved a similar hip pattern.*

One of the earliest diapsids was a *Petrolacosaurus* from the late Carboniferous. This creature was small, lithely built for hunting insects, and indicative of diapsid evolution for the next 40 million years, when synapsids dominated the landscape to the virtual exclusion of other reptiles. One of the more interesting diapsid exceptions, however, was the gliding *Coelurosauravus*, which used its elongated, membrane-covered ribs much as a modern flying squirrel uses the skin between its legs, while sailing from one tree to another.

Mass extinctions at the end of the Permian period, however, tipped the balance against the synapsids in favour of the diapsids, which responded with an explosion of evolutionary vigour. The most important (and most famous) group to appear were the archosaurs. This group was made up of the dinosaurs, crocodilians and pterosaurs.

Dinosaurs are divided into two broad categories, based on the shape of the hip – one of the seemingly insignificant differences upon which most of biological classification rests. One group, the ornithischians, had bird-like hips, while the other group, the saurischians, had a more reptilian hip (the

differences are so striking that for decades, the two groups were ranked as taxonomic orders, in the belief that they arose from different ancestors).

The ornithischians, or beaked dinosaurs, include many of the best-known herbivorous dinosaurs: the stegosaurs, the ceratopsians like *Triceratops*, the ankylosaurs, and the hadrosaurs, or duck-billed dinosaurs. The saurischians get the glory, however, with such theropods as *Deinonychus, Tyrannosaurus* and *Allosaurus*, and sauropods like *Apatosaurus, Mamenchisaurus* with its 35-foot/10.5 metre neck, and the incredible *Seismosaurus* from New Mexico, which may have stretched 140 feet/40 metres in length.

The end of the Cretaceous period 65 million years ago marked another mass extinction, perhaps brought on by a comet or asteroid striking the Earth. Whatever the cause, the dinosaurs died out, with the exception of their descendants, the birds. Many other diapsids, however – lizards, turtles, crocodilians and the recently evolved snakes – survived the cataclysm that claimed the dinosaurs, and continue to enrich the natural world.

# TURTLES AND TORTOISES

The shell of a turtle may be the most remarkable armour any land animal has evolved. At its most sophisticated, as in the box turtles common in North America, the shell is of two parts – a domed "carapace" above, with a flatter "plastron" on the underside, hinged a third of the way back. When threatened, the box turtle pulls its legs, tail and head inside and closes up the shell. The seal is almost perfect in the front, and although a determined predator may be able to nip the slightly exposed tail and hind legs, the turtle is usually safe.

Turtles are among the oldest group of surviving reptiles, having evolved at some point prior to the Triassic period, when their fossils first appear in rock strata. The carapace shell is actually highly modified ribs, which expanded and fused into the solid, bony armour; one small reptile from the Permian, *Eunotosaurus*, shows what might have been an intermediate step in turtle evolution, with paddle-shaped ribs inside the body providing protection for the internal organs.

The earliest true turtles, however, would be instantly recognizable as such. *Proganochelys*, from the Triassic, is a good example – a prehistoric turtle complete with carapace, plastron and horny beak. Another famous fossil species, the Cretaceous' *Archelon*, shows the progression of turtles into another direction, the sea.

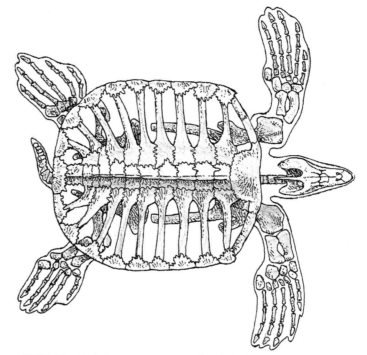

**ABOVE: The *Archelon* was a huge turtle that swam the Cretaceous seas. From nose to tail it was about 15 ft/5 m long, but swam in much the same way as smaller modern turtles.**

**BELOW: The shell of a turtle – in this case, the algae-covered dome of a Florida red-bellied turtle – may well be the most remarkable armour ever evolved by a vertebrate.**

Sea turtles apparently split from the terrestrial and freshwater stock early in turtle evolution, and have become highly specialized for life in the open ocean. *Archelon*, like the modern sea turtles, had a flattened, streamlined shape very unlike a land-dwelling turtle's; the legs were modified into flattened paddles, which in modern sea turtles are flapped, much as a bird's wings in flight, propelling the turtle swiftly through the water. The greatest difference between *Archelon* and modern sea turtles is size – *Archelon* was almost 13 feet/4 metres long, while most living species of sea turtles are half that.

There are surviving giants, however. The leatherback turtle, found worldwide, is the heaviest reptile in the world, 11 feet/3.3 metres long and weighing almost a ton(ne); it is so massive that it can maintain a constant body temperature even in cold northern waters, making it at least nominally "warm-blooded". In freshwater, the alligator snapping turtle of the Mississippi basin attains weights of more than 300 pounds/136 kilograms.

**ABOVE: Even the most ancient fossil turtles so far discovered resemble modern species; the** extinct *Proganochelys*, **for example, looked much like this snapping turtle.**

## SNAPPING TURTLES

While massive sea turtles are accomplished swimmers, the alligator snapping turtle is lethargic and cumbersome – yet it eats fish, a particularly agile prey. How can a predator so slow manage to catch something so fast?

The answer is that the snapping turtle is an ambush hunter. Its jagged shell and dull coloration blends well with the river bottom making the turtle hard to see. When in position the turtle opens its mouth and wriggles a small, pink finger of flesh on the floor of the mouth. Fish, seeing what they mistake for a worm, come close with a view to feeding – and discover that the two things a snapping turtle can move quickly are its head and jaws.

31

# CROCODILIANS

There may be no more ancient-looking group of reptiles in the world than the alligators, crocodiles and their relatives, known collectively as crocodilians. Looks aside, however, crocodiles are neither the living descendants of the dinosaurs, as is often thought, nor are they the oldest branch of the reptiles, since turtles and lizards pre-date them considerably.

Today, there are 22 species of living crocodilians, found in tropical and subtropical habitats around the world. They range from the tiny West African dwarf crocodile, barely 6 feet/1.8 metres long, to the saltwater crocodile of southeast Asia and Australia, which has been recorded as growing up to 28 feet/8.4 metres long.

Most crocodilians fall between these extremes. One of the best known, the American alligator, averages 8 to 10 feet/2.4 to 3 metres in length, with 19 feet/5.7 metres the largest on record.

Crocodilians are relatively advanced reptiles, with the most dramatic difference being the structure of the heart. Instead of the inefficient, three-chambered heart of most reptiles, crocodiles have a four-chambered heart, which separates oxygen-rich blood from oxygen-depleted blood that has already flowed through the body.

Crocodilians arose in the late Permian period from the same ancestral stock that a few million years later gave rise to the dinosaurs, and they share a number of dinosaur-like features, including the structure of the teeth and hips. Among the earliest animals in this line were the Erythrosuchidae, the so-called "crimson crocodiles" because of the red rock in which the first fossils were found. Big, agile land predators, the crimson

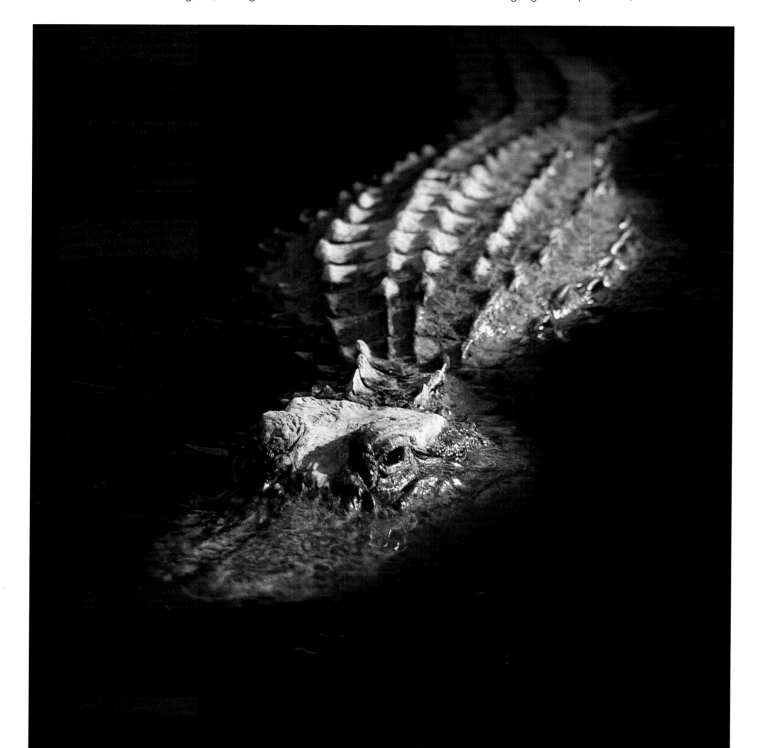

ABOVE: Worldwide there are 22 species of crocodilians; this South American species, the spectacled caiman, is one of the smaller members, reaching about 7 feet/2.1 metres at maturity.

RIGHT: A Nile crocodile at the Samburu Game Reserve in Kenya feeds on a captured impala; unlike some prehistoric crocodiles, crocodilians today are mostly ambush hunters.

LEFT: An alligator, floating in a peat-stained river, looks unimaginably ancient, but is really a member of a fairly recent branch of the reptiles.

# PARASUCHUS

*The Triassic crocodylotarsan Parasuchus is well known from a number of nearly complete skeletons. It looked, and probably behaved, like a typical modern freshwater crocodilian, preying on fish and small and medium-sized animals at the waterside. But crocodylotarsans are not in fact ancestors of modern crocodilians, but evolved their features independently, as can be shown by detailed study. For example, the long snout of Parasuchus is formed from different bones to those in the snouts of crocodilians.*

crocodiles were far from our normal image of crocodilians; some later species even evolved into cumbersome, heavily armoured herbivores.

The dawn of the Triassic period brought changes for the crimson crocodiles, which split into two major groups – the crocodylotarsans and the ornithosuchians. The former gave rise to true crocodilians, the latter to dinosaurs and birds.

One of the early crocodylotarsans, *Parasuchus*, dates back to the Triassic period. It was a freshwater hunter from Asia and would have looked very much like a modern crocodile – with a long tail, short legs and an elongated snout studded with teeth. Its skeletal structure, especially the skull, is different, however – another example of how environmental pressures can lead to similar body shapes in animals that are not closely related.

True crocodilians had evolved by the Triassic, beginning as small, terrestrial insectivores before moving to the marine habitats that mark the group to this day. The tail became increasingly powerful, with vertebral prongs sprouting vertically and horizontally to anchor the muscles and provide additional support – all helping to propel the creature through the water.

An exception to the aquatic lifestyles of the ancient crocodilians is *Pristichampus*. This 10-foot/3-metre crocodile from the Eocene epoch hunted mammals on the open plains. All crocodiles can run rapidly in short bursts, but *Pristichampus* evolved longer than average legs and strong claws for traction, suggesting that it was capable of running down many of the smaller mammals that shared its world.

# MONITOR LIZARDS

On the tiny Indonesian island of Komodo, where the climate is searingly hot and arid, the largest lizards in the world live – so huge they have earned the name "dragons". The Komodo dragon is a monitor lizard, similar to the monitors of Africa and Australia. But most of those species are a few feet long and eat snails, while the Komodo dragon can exceed 9 feet/2.7 metres, and hunts goats, water buffalo and other large mammals.

As impressive as a Komodo dragon is – and a full-grown adult, capable of sprinting fast enough to overtake its warm-blooded prey, is *very* impressive – there were much larger monitors in the recent past. Paleontologists in Australia have uncovered the remains of giant goannas (as monitors are known there) that reached lengths of 21 feet/6.4 metres and weights of up to 1,300 pounds/591 kilograms.

The giant goannas, of the genus *Megalania*, survived through the Pleistocene, when Australia was largely covered by grassy plains. As in other parts of the world, the Australian Pleistocene was a time of giant animals, including a species of now-extinct, short-faced kangaroo that stood 8 feet/2.4 metres tall and weighed more than 600 pounds/273 kilograms.

Like its modern relative the Komodo dragon, *Megalania* apparently also hunted active, warm-blooded prey, including short-faced kangaroos and other fast-running marsupials; scientists suspect the monster lizards also fed on carrion, which would have been abundant on the plains.

No one is certain why the giant goanna died out in Australia just a few thousand years ago, but its extinction coincided with the disappearance of the rest of the island continent's larger wildlife. Scientists have found thick deposits of salty dust, dating from 26,000 and 6,000 years ago, that indicate huge dust storms – perhaps the result of epic droughts. Such climatic changes might well have doomed the giant mammals, and with them such predators as *Megalania*.

For whatever reason, the Komodo dragon has survived in its Indonesian hideaway, with between 2,500 and 5,000 on the islands of Komodo, Rintja, Gillimontang and Flores. Protected by local law, international treaty and the extreme remoteness of the islands, the dragons are nevertheless at risk, since they occupy a very restricted range.

**LEFT: Stretching high, a lace monitor lizard surveys the Australian scrub where it makes its home.**

# PLOTOSAURUS

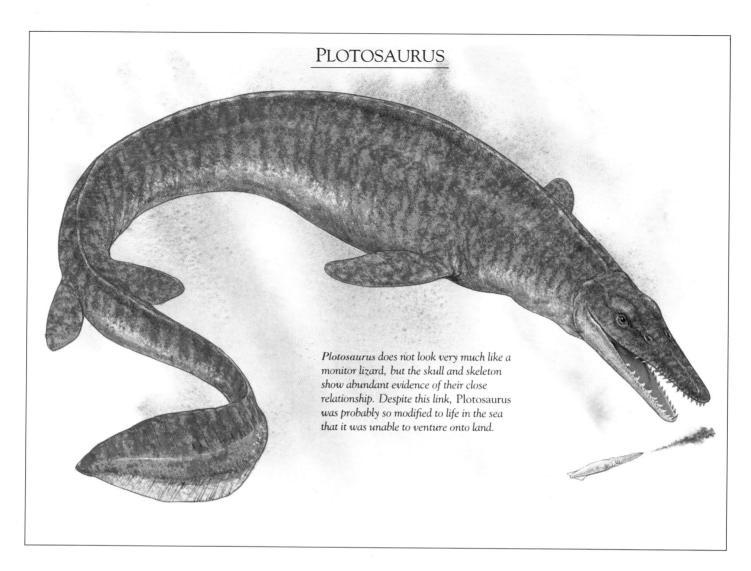

*Plotosaurus does not look very much like a monitor lizard, but the skull and skeleton show abundant evidence of their close relationship. Despite this link, Plotosaurus was probably so modified to life in the sea that it was unable to venture onto land.*

**RIGHT: A monitor lizard climbing a tree, perhaps in search of birds' eggs, pauses to survey its surroundings.**

# SNAKES

Everything we do in life involves our hands, so it is hard for humans to imagine a successful strategy that involves *losing* one's limbs. Yet snakes have taken just such a course, abandoning their legs long ago – and with spectacular results.

Today, there are more than 2,300 species of snakes in the world, in almost every conceivable habitat, from tropical rain forests to arid deserts to temperate meadows. There are even marine seasnakes that never set foot – or at least belly – on land. Only extreme cold defeats their reptilian metabolisms, but even so, a few very hardy species are found living just north of the Arctic Circle.

Snake remains are few and far between in the fossil record, in large part because snake bones are thin and delicate, unlike the rugged skulls of many mammals. Enough snake fossils have been found, though, to make it clear that snakes branched off from lizards in the early Cretaceous period.

A snake is more than just a lizard without legs, however; the differences go deeper than a lack of limbs. Because a snake's body is so strongly compressed, there have been major alterations in internal organs – the left lung in most species has withered to a tiny vestige, as have one of each of the kidneys and oviducts. The eyelid has been replaced by a fixed, transparent scale, and the external ear has vanished.

In order to move, a snake can call on a complicated arrangement of muscles, ribs and scales that permits a stately caterpillar crawl, with each overlapping belly scale sliding fractionally forward, gripping the ground and pulling the rest of the body on behind. For faster movement, though, snakes rely on serpentine motion, the classic S-curves that anchor the body against even the tiniest irregularities in the ground and push the snake forward. On an especially loose surface, such as sand, the snake can "sidewind", moving sideways by throwing successive loops of its body forwards.

With all the changes snakes have undergone, there are still some visible links to their past. On a number of primitive groups, like the boas and pythons, you can find tiny, conical spurs on either side of the male's vent (urinogenital opening), which are vestigial limbs, with a remnant pelvic girdle inside the body, hearkening back to a day when snakes had limbs.

Scientists speculate that snake ancestors may have been burrowers, since many modern burrowing lizards are legless, or nearly so. Legs would be a hindrance to a creature that spends most of its time below the surface, but snakes apparently found leglessness a decided advantage above ground, too, and in the course of the past 150 million years they have dispersed into a huge variety of ecological niches.

**RIGHT: Pulling itself into a defensive posture, a juvenile Bismark ringed python threatens an intruder. Snakes have made a success of what would seem to be a liability – the lack of limbs.**

**OPPOSITE: A yellow rat snake swallows all but the last of a rat, made possible by flexible jaws that unhinge, permitting the snake to swallow whole food larger than its head.**

**LEFT: Its tail buzzing furiously, a western rattlesnake warns away predators with its unique rattles – actually modified, loosely jointed scales.**

**BELOW: Pit vipers like this northern copperhead have a deep pit between the eye and nostril, lined with heat-sensing cells that allow the copperhead to track its prey in the dark.**

## PIT VIPERS

The pinnacle of snake evolution are the pit vipers, a large group possessing a sophisticated venom-injection system, and an incredibly effective heat-sensing pit on either side of the head.

Unlike the cobras, coral snakes and seasnakes, pit vipers possess hinged fangs, which swing forward from the roof of the mouth before striking. The long fangs are hollow, acting like hypodermic needles, and are connected to two venom glands behind the eye and jaw. Sensing the heat of a mouse or other small prey animal, the snake calculates the distance and strikes. The snake then waits until the venom has had time to kill the prey and then tracks it down and eats it.

BIRDS

# THE DINOSAURS THAT DID NOT DIE

It remains one of the most electrifying fossils in the world, more than 130 years after it came out of a German limestone quarry: a lightly built skeleton with long legs and tail, a supple neck and a snouted skull with teeth, unmistakably a dinosaur. And yet, around the arms and tail, the clear impressions of feathers – unmistakably a bird. It is *Archaeopteryx*, and its discovery made science rethink the relation between birds and reptiles.

Scientists long suspected that birds evolved from reptiles – their shared habits of laying eggs, similarities in ankle position, the structure of the skull, ears and jaws, even the presence of scales on bird legs, made that clear. But what reptiles gave rise to birds, and when?

Today, the debate is between those who stick with the traditional view, that birds evolved from thecodonts, ancestors of the dinosaurs and crocodilians, and those who believe birds sprang directly from dinosaurs. This latter viewpoint has been greatly strengthened by recent discoveries, particularly studies of the predatory dinosaur *Deinonychus*, which is eerily bird-like in almost every important respect, from the construction of its wrists to the shape of its shoulder and ankle.

It now seems likely that birds are the direct descendants of the highly evolved dinosaurs; in fact, this lends a great deal of weight to arguments that the dinosaurs themselves were warm-blooded and active, rather than the plodding, cold-blooded creatures always portrayed. Some paleontologists now see no reason why dinosaurs like *Deinonychus* could not have enjoyed an insulating coat of feathers, too.

The development of feathers from scales is not, incidentally, as great an evolutionary leap as it might seem. Feathers and scales are made of the same general group of substances, and most avian paleontologists believe feathers arose through a process of scale enlargement and fraying, eventually leading to the secondary splits and connecting hooklets that are seen in modern feathers.

Unfortunately, bird fossils are not common, most likely because bird bones are thin and hollow, easily destroyed by weather and decomposition. *Archaeopteryx* is a clear link

## ARCHAEOPTERYX

Archaeopteryx ("ancient wing") is arguably the most famous fossil of all. The first specimen was a feather, found in 1860. Since then, six skeletons have been collected. All specimens were found in the vicinity of Solnhofen in southern Bavaria, Germany. The fine-grained quality of the stone in this area has preserved numerous fossils beautifully, often with the soft parts of the original animal or plant still visible. This is ideal stone for preserving the delicate bones and feathers of Archaeopteryx. The fossils show several characteristics unique to birds today, such as feathers, a particular wing structure and joined clavicles (the "wishbone").

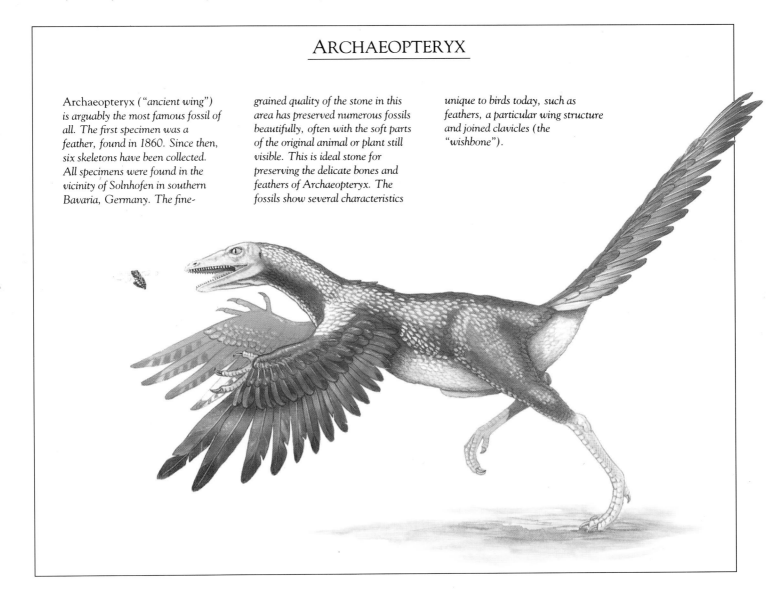

between dinosaurs and true birds, suggesting that by the late Jurassic and early Cretaceous periods bird evolution was in full swing, but the fossil record is patchy.

There are several fossil birds that stand out. During the Cretaceous, what would eventually become the western part of the United States was covered by a shallow, weed-choked sea, perfect for seabirds. A group of primitive birds that thrived in this time and place were the hesperornithiformes, of which 13 species are known. Flightless, with long necks and powerfully built hind legs, they probably dived for fish much as modern cormorants do today – but unlike today's cormorants, they possessed reptilian jaws complete with teeth set in sockets.

Another famous Cretaceous bird was *Ichthyornis*, a small, delicately built creature that may have filled the niche now taken by terns and gulls – although it, too, was the possessor of a mouthful of teeth.

The toothed birds of the Cretaceous died out during the mass extinctions that marked the beginning of the Tertiary period about 65 million years ago, but during the Eocene epoch that followed, modern birds blossomed, including such familiar groups as ducks, gulls, cranes and cormorants.

## FLIGHT IN THE ARCHAEOPTERYX

Few scientists now doubt that *Archaeopteryx* is an ancestor (or a close relative of the ancestor) of modern birds. Today, the biggest arguments are over how flight first evolved, and how much flying ability *Archaeopteryx* had.

Its strong hind legs suggest that *Archaeopteryx* was an accomplished runner, much as modern turkeys are, but the small breastbone provides a poor anchor for the sort of muscles modern birds need to fly, and it seems likely that *Archaeopteryx* could flap weakly, at best.

There are two theories on how the forerunners to birds (protobirds) first took to the air – the "arboreal" and "cursorial". According to arboreal theory, the protobirds were tree-dwelling creatures that used their feathers and primitive wings for gliding between trees. The cursorial theory, on the other hand, suggests that the bird-like dinosaurs used their wings to gain extra height when leaping off the ground to capture prey or escape enemies.

The truth, many paleontologists believe, may lie in a marriage of the two views, since a protobird might very well have needed the ability to glide from trees *and* leap of the ground. Most likely, we will never know for certain.

# THE ORIGIN OF BIRDS

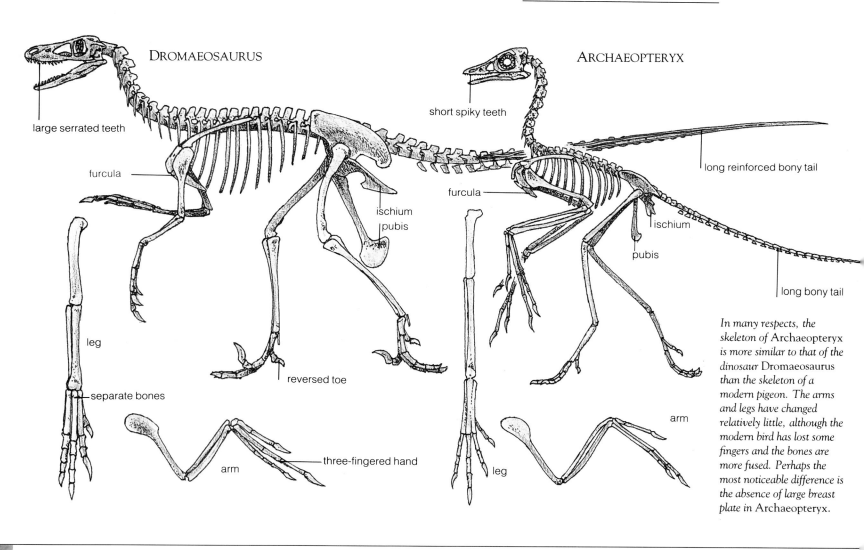

DROMAEOSAURUS

ARCHAEOPTERYX

large serrated teeth

furcula

ischium
pubis

leg

separate bones

reversed toe

arm

three-fingered hand

short spiky teeth

long reinforced bony tail

furcula

ischium

pubis

long bony tail

arm

leg

*In many respects, the skeleton of Archaeopteryx is more similar to that of the dinosaur Dromaeosaurus than the skeleton of a modern pigeon. The arms and legs have changed relatively little, although the modern bird has lost some fingers and the bones are more fused. Perhaps the most noticeable difference is the absence of large breast plate in Archaeopteryx.*

**LEFT:** During the Cretaceous period, a number of species of toothed water birds inhabited the shallow inland sea that covered what are now the North American plains. Following a similar lifestyle is this anhinga, a modern toothless bird of the American tropics.

**OVERLEAF:** Flying repiles of the late Jurassic. Many pterosaurs, like *Anurognathus* (bottom right), were tiny; *Rhamphorhynchus* (left) and *Pterodactylus* (top right;), were about the size of seagulls; and the earliest known bird, *Archeopteryx* (middle left) was about the size of a pigeon.

**BELOW:** The Eocene epoch saw the development of a number of modern bird families, including the ducks.

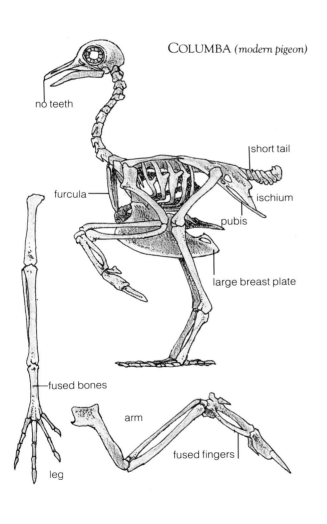

COLUMBA (*modern pigeon*)

- no teeth
- short tail
- furcula
- ischium
- pubis
- large breast plate
- fused bones
- arm
- fused fingers
- leg

The Eocene also boasted some decidedly unfamiliar birds as well. Perhaps the most spectacular were the diatrymas, massively built, flightless hunters of the North American plains, with thick legs and robustly hooked beaks. Considering that some diatrymas stood about 7 feet/2 metres tall, they must have been a thoroughly imposing presence among their smaller mammalian neighbours.

The Quaternary period, which produced such mammalian giants as the mammoths and cave bears, also gave rise to a number of avian giants, among them the flightless moas and elephant birds, and the monstrous condors that lived in the Western Hemisphere.

## TOOTHED BIRDS

Charles Darwin's theory on evolution, showing how natural selection could slowly change one type of organism into another, set off shock waves in the nonscientific community, although most scientists had long before accepted the idea of evolution. Attacked by conservatives and church leaders, vocal evolutionists like Thomas Henry Huxley could not have been more delighted by the announcement by Yale professor Charles Marsh, in 1880, that he had discovered fossils of birds with teeth.

Marsh's discoveries, coming from Cretaceous fossil beds in Kansas, provided powerful proof for the relationship between birds and reptiles – and a persuasive argument in favour of evolution. Ironically, Huxley was the first person to propose that birds were the direct descendants of dinosaurs, a theory that was ignored for almost a century but is now widely accepted as being correct.

Rhamphorhynchus

Pterodactylus

Anurognathus

Archaeopteryx

# THE FLIGHTLESS RATITES

The ratites are perhaps the most unbirdlike of all the birds — the towering ostrich of Africa and the smaller rhea of South America, Australia's emu, the bizarre cassowary of New Guinea and Australia, with its bright blue-and-red head and keel-shaped helmet, and the almost mammalian kiwi of New Zealand are all examples of ratites.

Ratites are all flightless, with the heavy, thickened legs of professional runners; this is especially true of the plains dwellers like ostriches and rheas, which can hit speeds of 30 to 40 miles per hour/50 to 65 kilometres per hour, and sustain them for long periods of time. The toes have been reduced to two in ostriches and three in rheas, emus and cassowaries.

The three species of cassowary are also strong runners, even though they are rain-forest creatures; the cone-like casque on the cassowary's head is thought to help it bull through tangled brush. The cassowary may well be the world's most dangerous bird, with an aggressive temper and razor-sharp inner toenails. If angered, a cassowary can lash out with accurate kicks, and there have been many cases of humans killed by being disemboweled or receiving other serious injuries.

Most of the ratites retain vestigial wings that are used as a rudder when running and for displays, as is the case with the ostrich. Kiwis and cassowaries have taken flightlessness even further, having virtually lost both wings; cassowaries have only a few remnant wing quills that deflect thorns from the body.

The three species of kiwis are fascinating for a number of reasons, including their burrowing habits and their relatively enormous eggs as much as a quarter of the female's mass, compared to about 8 per cent for most birds.

It is thought that the ratites branched off from the main avian

stock while the Gondwanaland supercontinent (which broke up to form the southern continents) was still joined; this would explain the presence of closely related, flightless birds scattered across the Southern Hemisphere.

Many of the surviving ratites are large (the ostrich is the most massive bird in the world), but during the Pleistocene epoch some veritable giants appeared. In New Zealand, as many as 20 species of moas evolved, birds related to kiwis but built like ostriches, with long legs and giraffe-like necks that ended almost 10 feet/3 metres above the ground. In Madagascar the elephant birds evolved, a group that, while not as tall as the moas, was bulkier, weighing over half a ton(ne).

Sadly, everything we know about these remarkable birds comes from skeletons, for elephant birds and moas became extinct within the relatively recent past – moas just a hundred years before Europeans reached New Zealand, judging from radiocarbon dating. It seems likely that pressure from aboriginal hunters wiped out these relics of the Pleistocene, leaving us nothing but their bones at which to wonder.

## ELEPHANT BIRD EGGS

One of the most remarkable things about the extinct elephant birds of Madagascar was their positively enormous eggs. The largest so far found would have held about 2 gallons/9 litres of liquid in a shell almost 14 inches/35 centimetres long. By contrast, the smallest hummingbird eggs are less than a half-inch/ 1 centimetre long – and it would take more than 30,000 of these eggs to amount to the volume of just one single elephant bird egg.

# HOATZINS: THE "LINK" THAT ISN'T

Sliding through the flooded jungle of the Amazon basin, weaving around buttressed kapok trees and palm trunks festooned with spines, you come at last to a quiet oxbow lake, studded with giant lilypads and their huge, pink flowers. Sitting quietly in the dugout canoe as the ripples die away, you listen – and a strange noise comes from the trees around you. *Hwa-a-a-a! Hwa-a-a-a!* The breathy, indignant call echoes around the tiny lake, until at last you see the bird making it. And what a bird – a big, pheasant-like body, long tail, a ragged crest, and red eyes surrounded by bright blue skin.

This oddity is the hoatzin (pronounced "what-sin"), found only in the swampy forests of the Amazon drainage. Hoatzins are so strange that no one is quite sure where they fit in on the bird family tree; until recently they were lumped with the pheasants and curassows, but new biochemical studies suggest they are more closely related to cuckoos.

Almost everything about a hoatzin is surpassingly strange. It is virtually the only bird in the world to feed exclusively on leaves, and the only one to ferment them in a large, specialized crop (part of the intestine) that functions like a cow's ruminating stomach. But what captured scientific attention for years was the baby hoatzin's claws.

At hatching, a young hoatzin possesses two claws on each wing, at the tips of long, jointed bones. With these claws, the chick can scramble through the tangle of vines and palm spines in which the species nests, escaping predators (it will also dive unhesitatingly into the water, clinging below the surface until danger passes). As the chick ages, however, the claws disappear and the bones fuse together for strength in flight, as in other birds.

With its claws, unfused "fingers" and swivelling wrist, a young hoatzin's wing structure is remarkably similar to that of *Archaeopteryx* – so similar that it was once thought this species was a primitive link between *Archaeopteryx* and modern birds, and some reconstructions of *Archaeopteryx* even showed it with hoatzin-like plumage.

This is now known to be false; hoatzins are fairly advanced, despite their appearance, and the chicks' claws are an example of an evolutionary throwback, the resurrecting of an ancient structure to fit a modern need. Natural selection allowed hoatzins to reactivate the genetic code for flexible digits and claws, which all birds carry within their genes – not because hoatzins are primitive, but because evolution uses all the tools at its disposal to fit the organism to the environment.

**LEFT: Although they lose them before adulthood, hoatzin chicks possess wing claws and joints that are startlingly like those of *Archaeopteryx*.**

# THE LESSON OF THE FINCHES

Isolation is one of the most potent forces for evolution, since it cuts off the flow of genes between different populations. Nowhere is that more apparent than on islands, where isolation has created a host of "endemics", species found nowhere else.

The most famous endemics – and those with the greatest impact on evolutionary theory – are the 14 species of small, drab finches of the Galapagos Islands, stranded in the cold Pacific nearly 600 miles/960 kilometres off the coast of Ecuador in South America. Although all 14 species obviously sprang from the same ancestral stock, they have spread out over the islands, filling a host of ecological niches – a fact noted by Charles Darwin during his visit to the islands and which weighed heavily in formulating his theories of natural selection.

A niche is the unique combination of habitat, food and lifestyle that a living organism occupies. Because the Galapagos Islands are so far from the South American mainland, many niches were unoccupied when the ancestors of the Darwin finches blew in, probably on a storm. Biologists guess this ancestral species was a seed-eating ground finch, similar to many genera still found on the Pacific coast.

Travel over water, even among the relatively closely spaced islands of the Galapagos archipelago, is difficult for a small ground bird, so it may have taken a while for the finches to spread throughout the Galapagos, with residents of each island thus becoming further isolated. Cut off from the mainland and each other, the island populations evolved in different directions, filling the many unoccupied niches which would, on the mainland, have been filled by birds of other families.

There are several species of ground-dwelling, seed-eating finches with massive, nutcracker bills, but there are also cactus specialists and a large group of seed-eaters that live in trees; there are also tree-dwelling, insect-feeding finches that have developed slim bills like warblers, and one remarkable species that uses its bill to break open wood, then snaps off a cactus spine which it uses to skewer any insect hidden within.

The strangest of these birds by far, however, is the species of Darwin finch found living on Wenman Island. To supplement its diet, it has taken to pecking at the wings of boobies and drinking the seabirds' blood – the only case of vampirism that has been discovered in the bird world.

**TOP RIGHT: The Galapagos giant tortoise, like Darwin finches, is unique to the Galapagos Islands. Furthermore, variations (for example, in shell structure) are found between the inhabitants on various islands, giving 14 distinct subspecies (although two are now extinct).**

**ABOVE RIGHT: Marine iguanas, camouflaged against the Galapagos rock, sun themselves. The species is unique to the Galapagos, but because they are able to swim between islands with relative ease (they swim out to sea to graze on algae) there are no subspecies.**

**LEFT: The Galapagos Islands have evolved unique species of animal because of their extreme isolation from the mainland. In addition, each island is isolated to a lesser degree from the others in the group and has some unique chararcteristics in its fauna.**

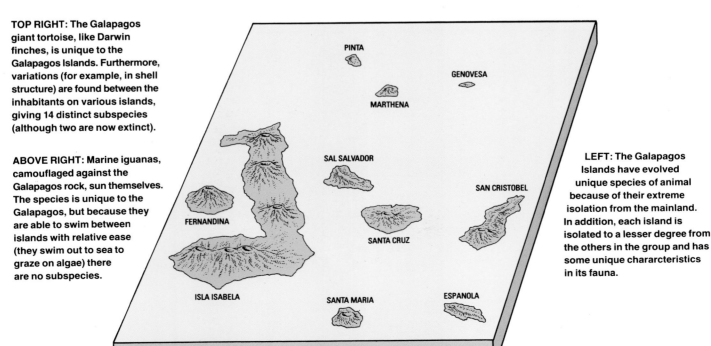

PINTA

GENOVESA

MARTHENA

SAL SALVADOR

SAN CRISTOBEL

FERNANDINA

SANTA CRUZ

ISLA ISABELA

SANTA MARIA

ESPANOLA

# THE THUNDERBIRDS OF THE AMERICAS

One of the most prevalent native legends in North America was that of the Thunderbird, a deity in the shape of a giant bird that carried the rains on its back, and sent the lightning crashing to Earth.

Until fairly recently, one did not have to look far to find the living embodiment of the Thunderbird. From British Columbia to Baja California, the California condor sailed the skies on wings stretching nearly 9 feet/2.7 metres from tip to tip. European colonization brought the condor's world to an end, however; within a century, it was restricted to a tiny section of rugged California mountain country, and in recent years has existed only in captivity.

To the south, the Andean condor, a slightly larger species, has fared somewhat better, inhabiting the mountains from Colombia to Cape Horn, hunting the arid highlands and coastal plain for carrion. Yet even these two imposing species pale beside several of their extinct Pleistocene cousins.

These were the giant condors known as teratorns, and they may well have been the biggest birds to ever take to the air. The best-known (and most intensely studied) was *Teratornis merriami*, which had a wingspan of about 13.5 feet/4.1 metres and apparently was common in western parts of America during the last ice age.

Its skeletons have been pulled from tar pits and show a spectacular wing breadth and heavy, hooked beak, but, like modern vultures, rather weak feet without talons – a strong indication that they fed on carrion. Most likely, the carcasses of large mammals attracted them to the pits, and they themselves became trapped in the naturally occurring petroleum, sank and were preserved.

*T. merriami* was by no means the largest of the teratorns. Another species, aptly named *T. incredibilis*, had a 20-foot/6-metre wingspan, and another from South America (based on a reconstruction of the wing bones) had a breathtaking span of more than 25 feet/7.5 metres.

The Pleistocene epoch was the perfect time for such carrion-eating giants, since the ice ages produced a wealth of massive mammals, most of them living on the plains, where thermal air currents are common and there are no trees to interfere with landings and takeoffs. With the mass extinctions of the large mammals that occurred, the teratorns' food supply was sharply reduced, and the largest species of birds ever to have flown also faded into extinction.

Even the smaller condors suffered setbacks. Fossil discoveries show that California condors were once found over most of North America, as far as New York and Florida, as recently as 11,000 years ago. They survived in western North America, feeding on elk, bison and deer carcasses, as well as beached whales and dead sea lions. When the Lewis and Clark expedition wintered along the Columbia River in 1805, their hunters were constantly bothered by condors eating the elk they shot before the meat could be taken back to camp.

# QUETZALCOATLUS

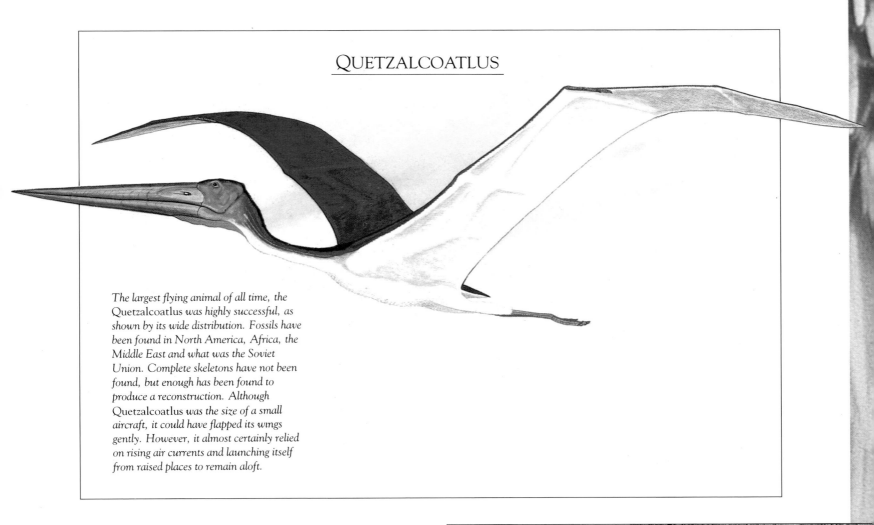

*The largest flying animal of all time, the Quetzalcoatlus was highly successful, as shown by its wide distribution. Fossils have been found in North America, Africa, the Middle East and what was the Soviet Union. Complete skeletons have not been found, but enough has been found to produce a reconstruction. Although Quetzalcoatlus was the size of a small aircraft, it could have flapped its wings gently. However, it almost certainly relied on rising air currents and launching itself from raised places to remain aloft.*

## THE LARGEST FLYING ANIMAL

The discovery of huge *Teratornis* remains in Argentina poses the question: how big can a flying animal become and still be able to fly?

With its 25-foot/7.5-metre wingspan, the largest teratorn was easily the largest known bird, but the group of flying dinosaurs known as pterosaurs easily eclipses it. As early as the 19th century, paleontologists discovered the remains of pterosaurs with wingspans of 20 feet/6 metres or more, but the most electrifying discovery wasn't made until the 1970s, when researchers in Texas came upon the wing and jaw bones of the biggest flying animal ever – *Quetzalcoatlus northropi*.

There has been considerable argument about the size of *Quetzalcoatlus*, with some estimates ranging as big as 65 feet/19.7 metres, but at a minimum it had a wingspan of 35 or 40 feet/10.6 or 12.1 metres, bigger than many small planes.

The laws of physics conspire against big flying animals; the amount of energy needed to fly escalates dramatically, while the efficiency of muscles decreases as they grow in size. It may well be that with *Quetzalcoatlus*, evolution reached the largest expression of living flight possible – but of course, that's what scientists used to say about 20-foot/6-metre pterosaurs.

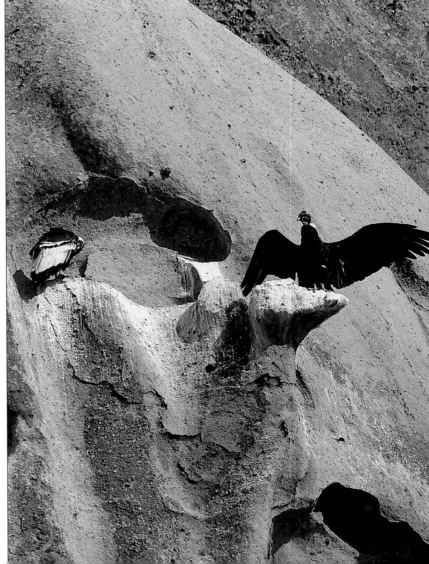

**LEFT: With a wingspan of 9 feet/ 2.7 metres, the Andean condor is one of the largest flying birds that is alive on Earth today.**

**RIGHT: An Andean condor stretches its wings from a perch beside its nest cave, in a weathered cliff face in Patagonia, South America.**

# DIFFERENT BEGINNINGS, SIMILAR ENDS

A point that is raised repeatedly in any discussion of animal evolution and ancestry is that appearances can be deceiving. Just because two animals happen to look alike, does not mean that they are closely related, or even that they share recent, common ancestors.

Birds provide a terrific example of this rule – the penguins of the Southern Hemisphere and the auks of the Northern Hemisphere, including murres and puffins. Both groups are generally stocky, largely black-and-white seabirds with legs far to the rear of the body, so they stand upright on land. Penguins are completely flightless and the auks are just barely able to become airborne; one species, in fact, the now-extinct great auk, was indeed flightless. Both groups feed on fish and aquatic invertebrates, usually captured in an underwater chase. Anyone would assume they were close relatives.

But looks, as we noted, are deceiving. Ornithologists believe that penguins are descended from birds known as tubenoses, which today include petrels and albatrosses – indeed, fossil penguins possessed that group's characteristic tubular nostrils, as does the fairy penguin, the most primitive living species. Auks, on the other hand, are thought to have evolved from gulls and their relatives, an entirely different order of birds from the tubenoses. Similar environmental pressures produced what is termed parallel evolution, in which the two groups evolved along similar lines.

According to this theory, borne out by biochemical analysis as well as fossils, both the penguins and auks passed through an intermediate stage in which the wings are reduced in size, but still function in the air and underwater for swimming. With the exception of the great auk, the rest of the auks have stayed at this stage, while in the southern oceans, diving petrels are thought to be similar to the penguin's ancestors.

Fossils show that penguins and auks had both diverged into distinct groups by the early Eocene, about 60 million years ago. The oldest fossil penguins are small, probably because their immediate ancestors were still able to fly, but once flight was no longer a survival requirement the penguins were free to increase in size. The largest of the species today is the emperor penguin, standing about 4 feet/1.2 metres tall and weighing about 90 pounds/40 kilograms.

Auks have remained much smaller, since all must labour into the air on frantically buzzing wings. The great auk, having given up flight entirely, like the penguins, was likewise able to grow to a much larger size, standing almost 30 inches/76 centimetres tall. Agile in the water, it was unable to escape humans on land, and its breeding colonies in the north Atlantic were systematically plundered for meat and eggs. The last great auk was seen in 1852.

**BELOW AND RIGHT:
Superficially similar, penguins and auks – in this case, Magellanic penguins from Argentina (below) and common** **guillemots from Scotland (right) – are really not closely related at all. Both groups have arrived at similar shapes because they live in similar environments.**

# DAY SHIFT, NIGHT SHIFT

By day, small mammals must avoid a host of predators, but none sharper-eyed than the daytime birds of prey – hawks, eagles and falcons. Then, at night, instead of getting a respite, the mice have to contend with owls, whose night-vision and excellent hearing allows them to hunt in almost total darkness.

Actually, the evolution of a day shift and night shift should come as no surprise. By evolving to hunt at different times, hawks and owls avoid direct competition with each other, thereby maximizing the number of ecological niches that are available to them.

For most diurnal (or daytime) niches, there is a complementary nocturnal niche when the sun goes down – and a comparable night-time hunter. In eastern North America, such "ecological analogues" are very much in evidence. By day, the American kestrel, a tiny falcon, hunts rodents,

insects and similar small prey; by night, many of the same creatures are hunted by the eastern screech-owl, just 8 inches/ 20 centimetres long. In wet woodlands, red-shouldered hawks hunt by day, feeding on small mammals, reptiles and amphibians; the night shift is taken by the barred owl. In fields and woodlots, the analogues are red-tailed hawks and great horned owls.

In addition to hooked beaks and powerful, taloned feet, owls have a number of adaptations specific to nocturnal hunting. The most impressive is their eyesight; the large eyes, which virtually fill the front of the skull, gather enormous amounts of light, permitting good vision in poor illumination.

What is less apparent, on first glance, is an owl's superior hearing. Barn owls, perhaps the most nocturnal of all owls, have been shown to be able to hunt in complete darkness,

**LEFT: In many habitats, hawks and owl share much the same resources, separated only by the time in which they hunt; in North America, the red-tailed hawk and great horned owl are two such ecological "analogues".**

**TOP RIGHT: A sharp, hooked beak is characteristic of hawks and owls; this is an immature goshawk, a common hunter in boreal forests of the Northern Hemisphere.**

**RIGHT: One of the most unusual owls is the northern hawk-owl, which with its daytime hunting habits, long tail and falcon-like flight is an oddity in its family.**

calculating the position of a mouse from the barely audible sounds of its movements. Many owls have asymmetrical ear openings, hidden beneath the facial feathers, for even more accurate targeting of their prey.

Fossils indicate that falconiforms (now consisting of hawks, falcons, ospreys and vultures) appeared in the late Eocene, making them one of the earliest groups to split off into a recognizable, modern order. Many of the genera still alive today, like *Buteo* (which includes the red-tailed hawk of North America and the common buzzard of Europe), can be traced back almost 30 million years, to the Oligocene, and both the booted eagles of the genus *Aquila* and the *Haliaeetus* sea eagles go back to the Miocene.

There is a great deal of controversy, however, over the origins of falconiforms, since the fossil record is incomplete, and leaves the question of ancestral stock unresolved. Some ornithologists believe the falconiforms arose from an ancient hawk similar to modern kites, while others argue that most hawks evolved from a raptor or vulture-like carrion eater with falcons arising from a different, nonraptorial ancestor.

The question of origins becomes even cloudier for owls. Once they were grouped as fairly close relatives of hawks, based on their predatory habits, but recent genetic analysis suggests they have more in common with nightjars.

MAMMALS

# MAMMALIAN EVOLUTION

## EARLY CYNODONTS

*The cynodonts were a group of mammal-like reptiles, first appearing in the Triassic. The early cynodonts were probably more immediately reminiscent of reptiles, while having some mammal characteristics.*

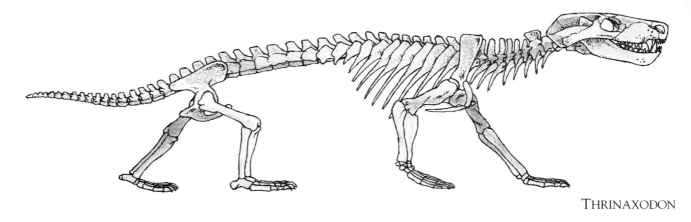

THRINAXODON

As we have seen, evolution does not proceed in a neat, straight line, from "primitive" organisms to "advanced" forms. Far from being a single trunk, evolution's course is more like a thicket, with twigs and branches shooting off in many directions, each with the potential to succeed.

When we consider mammals, for example, it is convenient to think of amphibians giving rise to reptiles, then reptiles giving way to mammals – and in a sense they did, but not in that neat and tidy order. The first mammals evolved at the dawn of the Age of Dinosaurs (248 million years ago), and their immediate ancestors were a distinct group during the Permian, in what is usually considered the Age of Amphibians.

Midway through the Permian period, a group of mammal-like reptiles, the forerunners of mammals, the protomammals or theraspids, first appeared; these were close relatives of the pelycosaurs, the most famous member of which was *Dimetrodon*, the massive, sailbacked reptile. The early protomammals were not sailbacked, however – they tended toward massive bodies and heavily armoured heads, which some paleontologists suggest were for head-butting bouts.

## PROBELESODON

*The later cynodonts probably looked so much like mammals that if they lived today, it would be hard to call them reptiles. There is a strong evidence that later cynodonts had hair and warm blood, for example, the bones of the snout show tiny pits for the nerves and blood vessels that served whiskers.*

# GEOLOGICAL TIME

The vast lengths of time involved in the history of the Earth and of life are hard to comprehend. It is difficult for someone to have a real sense of periods of time much longer than that of a human life. The Earth is more than 60-million human-lifetimes old.

Yet the enormous age of the Earth is an essential element in the life on the planet. Without the long lengths of time that have been available for life to evolve, there would not be the vast variety of complex life that we find today.

This is not because – as is sometimes thought – life has evolved purely by random chance and thus evolution has needed time for luck to work itself out in some sense. It is because life generally evolves in very small, gradual steps, generation by generation, working on tiny variations in individual organisms. To "put together" something as large and extraordinarily complex as, for example, an elephant in this way takes an enormously long time.

In order to gain an understanding of evolutionary processes, therefore, it is important to have a grasp of the timescales of Earth's history – or the geological timescale, as it is generally known. The scale is known as "geological" because it is closely linked to such things as the rocks that were being formed and their movements at various times in the Earth's development. Paleontology (the study of fossils) and the study of evolution have also played a major part in establishing the various divisions of the scale and their names.

The following pages open out to give a presentation of the geological timescale as it relates to the development of life. This is followed by a chart that gives a more conventional presentation of geological time.

# CHART OF THE GEOLOGICAL TIMESCALE

The figures in the chart indicate the number of years in millions before the present that the particular division starts.

| EON | | ERA | | PERIOD | | EPOCH | |
|---|---|---|---|---|---|---|---|
| PRECAMBRIAN | 4,600 | | | | | | |
| PHANEROZOIC | 565 | PALEOZOIC | 565 | CAMBRIAN | 565 | | |
| | | | | ORDOVICIAN | 500 | | |
| | | | | SILURIAN | 430 | | |
| | | | | DEVONIAN | 395 | | |
| | | | | CARBONIFEROUS | 345 | | |
| | | | | PERMIAN | 286 | | |
| | | MESOZOIC | 248 | TRIASSIC | 248 | | |
| | | | | JURASSIC | 213 | | |
| | | | | CRETACEOUS | 144 | | |
| | | CENOZOIC | 65 | TERTIARY | 65 | PALAEOCENE | 65 |
| | | | | | | EOCENE | 54 |
| | | | | | | OLIGOCENE | 37 |
| | | | | | | MIOCENE | 25 |
| | | | | | | PLIOCENE | 6 |
| | | | | QUATERNARY | 2 | PLEISTOCENE | 2 |
| | | | | | | HOLOCENE | 0.01 |

# AUSTRALIA'S MARSUPIAL MONSTERS

The early Cretaceous saw the great branching of mammalian evolution – one branch taking the placental approach to reproduction, the other a marsupial approach, in which the young are born shortly after conception, and subsequently raised in an enclosed pouch on the mother's body for the following weeks or months. Both groups seem to have evolved in the Western Hemisphere and spread quickly, since the world's continents were still largely joined.

Because placental mammals dominate the Earth today, it is tempting to think of marsupials as another evolutionary dead-end, but that is far from the truth. A marsupial lifestyle works very well, as substantiated by the survival of so many marsupial forms. Moreover, just before the boundary separating the Cretaceous and Tertiary periods, the marsupials were the dominant mammals, not the placentals.

Mass extinctions eliminated two of the three existing marsupial families, but even so, marsupials went on to be the most important in South America and Australia – and in Australia, the marsupial pre-eminence continues to this day.

Everyone is familiar with Australia's kangaroos, with their upright, humanistic stance and high-leaping abilities. What is less generally appreciated is that kangaroos are part of a wide pattern of convergent evolution among Australian mammals, in which the island continent's marsupials evolved in ways similar to placentals elsewhere, in order to fill similar niches.

The kangaroos, for instance, are the ecological counterparts of antelopes and gazelles elsewhere – fleet grazers of the open plains and brushland. There are dozens of other marsupial parallels, including sugar gliders that look (and sail) like placental flying squirrels, and the Tasmanian devil, similar in shape and habits to placental wolverines. There are marsupial "moles", "mice", even a marsupial "wolf", the thylacine, now presumed extinct.

The fossil record contains even more bizarre marsupials, especially from the Pleistocene, which was a time of giants in Australia as elsewhere. Short-faced kangaroos of the genus *Procoptodon* stood 8 feet/2.4 metres tall and weighed more than 600 pounds/273 kilograms, while a rhino-like marsupial, *Diprotodon*, was even heavier. A marsupial lion with opposable thumbs hunted the forests, although some scientists have argued that its heavy cutting teeth were used on fruits, not meat. Even kangaroos were not always what they seemed; one species was apparently carnivorous.

The large Australian mammals disappeared roughly 40,000 years ago, around the time of man's arrival on the continent, leading some to speculate that human hunting destroyed them. Others argue that climatic changes were the real killer, drying out Australia and sending the biggest species into decline.

**BELOW: Cut off from the fauna of other landmasses, Australia's marsupials evolved in parallel with placental mammals elsewhere.**

**Kangaroos, like these large greys, filled the grazing niche that, for example, was taken by antelopes and gazelles in Africa.**

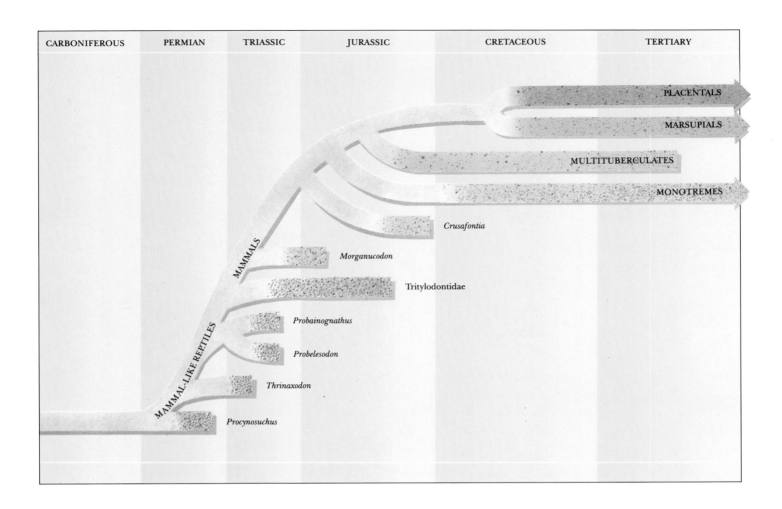

| CARBONIFEROUS | PERMIAN | TRIASSIC | JURASSIC | CRETACEOUS | TERTIARY |

PLACENTALS

MARSUPIALS

MULTITUBERCULATES

MONOTREMES

*Crusafontia*

*Morganucodon*

Tritylodontidae

*Probainognathus*

*Probelesodon*

*Thrinaxodon*

*Procynosuchus*

MAMMALS

MAMMAL-LIKE REPTILES

**ABOVE:** The chart illustrates the relationships between the main groups of mammals and mammal ancestors (which are discussed on previous pages). Of the three surviving groups, the monotremes (duck billed platypuses and spiny anteaters) are an ancient and more distantly related group. The marsupials and the placentals went their different ways during the Cretaceous.

**RIGHT:** Another example of Australia's extensive family of marsupials: a grizzled tree kangaroo.

**OVERLEAF:** Australia in the Pleistocene. One million years ago the grassy plains of southern Australia were dominated by marsupials, many of them giant forms of those alive today. The scene is reminiscent of the African plains, with marsupial "lions" (*Thylacoleo*) hunting down giant kangaroos (*Procoptodon*), which fill the niche of antelopes.

Procoptodon

Palorchestes

Zygomaturus

Thylacoleo

# TENACIOUS MARSUPIALS OF SOUTH AMERICA

There is persuasive evidence that marsupials first evolved in what is now South America, and that that continent was, for millions of years, a stronghold for marsupial evolution, cut off as it was from North America. As in Australia, marsupial counterparts of wolves, lions and many smaller forms evolved, even though placentals were present.

This changed drastically during the Pliocene, when the Central American land bridge formed between North and South America. Southern mammals moved north, and northern families south, but in the end the South American endemics lost, with many unique varieties becoming extinct, including all of the larger marsupials.

Opossums, however, survived the mass extinction, and today the New World tropics boast more than two dozen species. Most are small (the largest, the Virginia opossum, is the size of a house cat) and many are much smaller. The mouse opossums are a group of tiny, arboreal species that include the aptly named Emilia's gracile mouse opossum, just 8 inches/ 20 centimetres long – and more than half of that is slender tail. There is also a highly specialized water opossum with short, dense fur, webbed feet and a roughened surface to the palms for gripping fish.

Opossums are most successful in the tropics, but the Virginia opossum has taken the temperate zone by storm. Originally found from Central America through the southern United States, in the past two centuries it has steadily increased its range to the north, so that it is now found in New England, parts of southern Canada, the Midwest of the United States and along the Pacific coast as far as British Columbia. Its tropical heritage still shows, however; in the winter, it is prone to frostbite on its naked tail and ears.

**BELOW: The Virginia opossum is the most widespread and successful of the New World marsupials, the descendants of** a varied assemblage of marsupials that declined in the two million years after South America's isolation ended.

# BATS: THEME AND VARIATION

Few people spare much thought for bats because they are small and almost completely nocturnal. Moreover, because Western culture considers them creatures of evil omen, many people are actually quite scared of bats. Yet bats are among the most important of animals, making up a fifth of all mammalian species; they are also critically important from an ecological standpoint, since many species of tropical plant, including some trees, are pollinated only by bats.

developed sonar, and some insect- and fruit-eaters have flattened, leaf-shaped noses that help to generate the high-pitched sounds needed for echo-location. But the many various species of bats feed on equally varied food sources. The fringe-lipped bat, for example, feeds on frogs, the bulldog bat on fish snatched (in its elongated toes) from the water's surface, while a host of tropical bats feed on flower pollen, often with long, specialized tongues.

The finest collection of bats in the world can be found in Central and South America, where they have evolved to fill an impressive variety of ecological niches. It seems certain that the ancestral bat from which they are all descended was an insect-eater, probably similar to the *Myotis* bats of North America and Europe.

Today, there are usually as many species of bats in a given area of rain forest as all the other mammal species combined. Many of them are insect-eaters like their distant ancestors, but other families have spread out into a bewildering jumble of lifestyles, from eating fruit to drinking blood.

Insect-eating bats have exceptional echo-location abilities, finding and tracking their prey through bursts of ultrasonic sound, the echoes from which are picked up by their sensitive hearing. Many species of fruit-eating bats also have highly

**ABOVE: Mouth open, a little brown bat emits a constant stream of ultrasonic chirps, listening to the returning echoes to avoid obstacles and locate flying insects.**

The infamous vampire bat cuts tiny incisions in the limbs of sleeping mammals and laps – not sucks – the flowing blood; its legs and forearms are longer than in most bats, and it can walk easily while approaching a victim. The false vampire bat is a fearsome hunter, taking birds as large as cuckoos and trogons, while the small ghost bat, an insectivore, is pure white.

Bat fossils are rare, primarily because their bones are so fragile. The earliest bats known date from the Eocene epoch. They show an animal remarkably similar to modern species. Many scientists believe that bats must have evolved from some form of tree-climbing shrew, but the fossils to prove this theory have yet to be discovered.

# VARIATION IN BATS

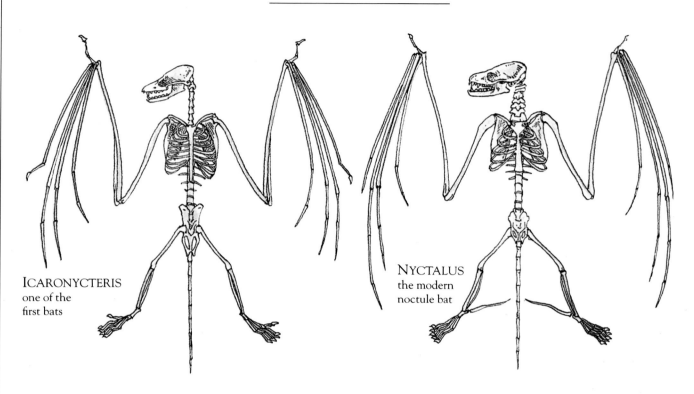

**ICARONYCTERIS**
one of the
first bats

**NYCTALUS**
the modern
noctule bat

The bat skeleton has not changed to any great degree during their known fossil history (above). We presume that bats had a tree-climbing shrew-like ancestor, but its fossils are not yet known. The skeleton has been modified for flight by lengthening the arm and fingers, to support the wing membrane, as well as thinning and lightening of other bones in order to reduce the overall bodyweight of the animal.

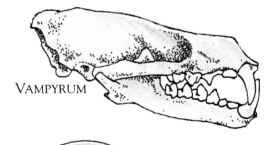

**VAMPYRUM**

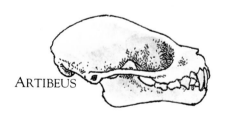

**ARTIBEUS**

**PHYLLOSTOMUS**

**ANOURA**

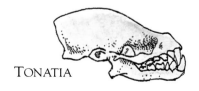

**TONATIA**

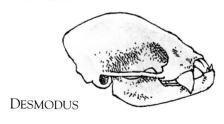

**DESMODUS**

Modern bats have various diets, reflected in their skull and tooth shapes. Five of these skulls (above) belong to the leaf-nosed group of bats, and the sixth to the vampire bat, Desmodus. Vampyrum feeds on flesh, Phyllostomus on flesh and plants, Tonatia on insects, Artibeus on fruit, Anoura on nectar, and Desmodus on blood.

# SLOTHS

Teeth can tell a biologist a great deal about an animal – its general size, its diet (and from that, much about its lifestyle), and for paleontologists another important aspect of teeth is that they are the hardest remains in a body, and the most likely to become fossilized.

The edentates, the group of primitive placental mammals that includes sloths, anteaters and armadillos, differ from other placentals by a number of skeletal and reproductive characteristics, but the biggest difference is their teeth – or the general lack of them. Anteaters, for example, have no teeth at all, just a long, tubular snout. Tree sloths, on the other hand, have only 18 teeth, really just simple pegs instead of the complicated molars found in many other mammals.

Sloths are a South American group with an amazing number of specialized adaptations for life in the trees. Slow-moving, they hang upside down from their long legs, which are tipped

**LEFT: Going through life in slow-motion, a brown-throated three-toed sloth carefully picks its way through the canopy of the South American rain forest, where it is one of the most common mammals.**

**BELOW: The mammals of South America evolved in isolation for most of the Tertiary period – about 60 million years. It was only about 3 million years ago that the Isthmus of Panama rose up and joined South and North America. A flood of mammals moved south from the North and north from the South.**

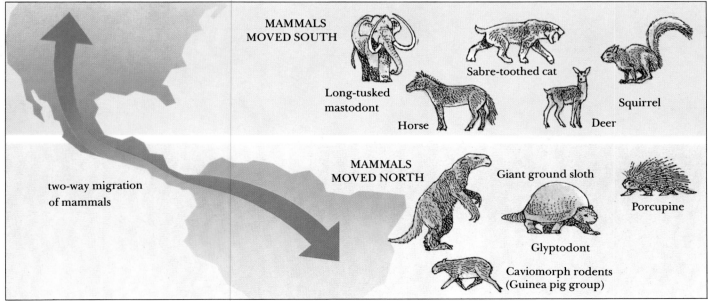

MAMMALS MOVED SOUTH

Long-tusked mastodont

Sabre-toothed cat

Horse

Deer

Squirrel

MAMMALS MOVED NORTH

two-way migration of mammals

Giant ground sloth

Porcupine

Glyptodont

Caviomorph rodents (Guinea pig group)

## MEGATHERIUM

*The giant sloth of South America is a quite recent loss to the world. Indeed, Megatherium has been extinct for only a few thousand years and preserved samples of hair and dung are still found. The dung was deposited in vast quantities in caves and other living quarters, and apparently one of these dung deposits in Argentina ignited and burned for six months! Megatherium has a broad, bowl-shaped pelvis, and it squatted like a tripod, balanced on its short hind legs and tail.*

with gracefully curving claws – three per foot in three species, and two per foot in the other two. Unlike other mammals, their hair grows from the stomach to the back, not the reverse. This is to help shed water when the animal hangs upside-down, and each hair has microscopic grooves in which algae grow, providing the sloth with a living camouflage coat.

Recent research shows that the three-toed and two-toed sloths are not as closely related as once thought; in fact, the two-toed sloth is now classified in the same family as its monstrous, extinct relative, the giant ground sloth *Megatherium. Megatherium* was one of the giants of the New

World ice ages; at nearly 20 feet/6 metres long it was the equivalent in size of a small elephant. Its hind legs were large and strong, its tail (a mere nub in modern sloths) long and presumably used as a brace when feeding on low trees; the curved claws of the front feet would have been used to grasp the vegetation it fed on.

Giant ground sloths only died out a few thousand years ago, and their mummified dung has been found in a number of South American caves – in a few cases so perfectly preserved that excited explorers felt certain there were living ground sloths still in the neighbourhood!

# ARMADILLOS AND GLYPTODONTS

What worked for the turtles has worked equally as well for the armadillos, namely living life in an armoured shell. But while a turtle's rigid dome is made up of specialized ribs, the curving plates on an armadillo's back are segments of highly evolved skin, rather than a rearranged skeleton.

There are 20 species of living armadillos, all from the New World, and all but one are restricted to Central and South America. The most widespread of the species, the nine-banded armadillo, is found from the southern plains of the United States to Argentina, and is named for the number of concentric armour rings that encase its body. Due to flexible skin between the plates, the nine-banded armadillo can curl itself into a protective ball, and its powerful forelegs and curved claws allow it to dig rapidly for shelter and food – the latter mostly ants

and termites. This same diet also supports the giant armadillo, which at 5 feet/1.5 metres in length and more than 120 pounds/54.5 kilograms is by far the biggest modern species.

There have been much larger armadillos in the past, however. During the Pliocene and Pleistocene epochs, a group known as glyptodonts thrived in South America. They were tank-like creatures as long as 11 feet/3.3 metres, and weighing more than two tonnes. Their shells were masterworks of small, interlocking plates, but unlike those of modern armadillos were not flexible. Archaeologists have unearthed glyptodont shells with the remains of fire hearths beneath them – evidence that Paleolithic humans used them for shelter.

Like other edentates, glyptodonts and their modern survivors had greatly reduced teeth, one of the characteristics of the group. *Glyptodon*, from North America, had just eight molars with which to bite and chew the plants it ate, while among armadillos the teeth are tiny pegs that are just sufficient for chewing insects.

**BELOW: The flexible armour bands on an armadillo provide protection while permitting** **easy movement; ancient armadillos like *Glyptodon* had inflexible shells.**

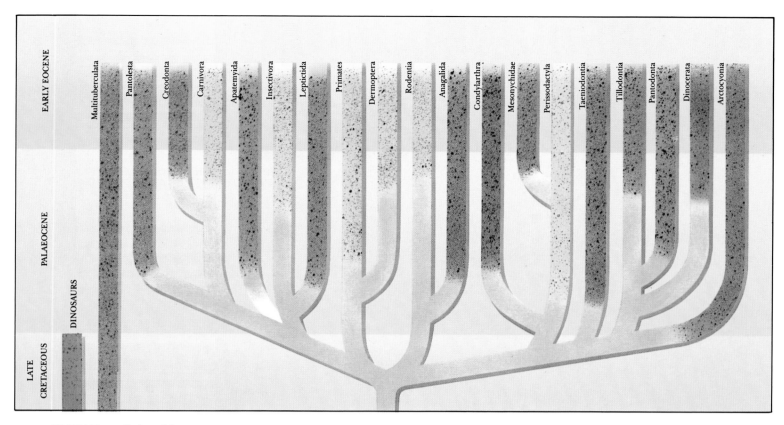

LATE CRETACEOUS

PALAEOCENE

EARLY EOCENE

DINOSAURS

Multituberculata
Pantolesta
Creodonta
Carnivora
Apatemyida
Insectivora
Leptictida
Primates
Dermoptera
Rodentia
Anagalida
Condylarthra
Mesonychidae
Perissodactyla
Taeniodontia
Tillodontia
Pantodonta
Dinocerata
Arctocyonia

**ABOVE: The radiation of the placental mammals in North** **America and Europe during the first 10 milion years of the age of** **the mammals. About 18 new groups arose, of which six** **survive today (indicated by lighter shading).**

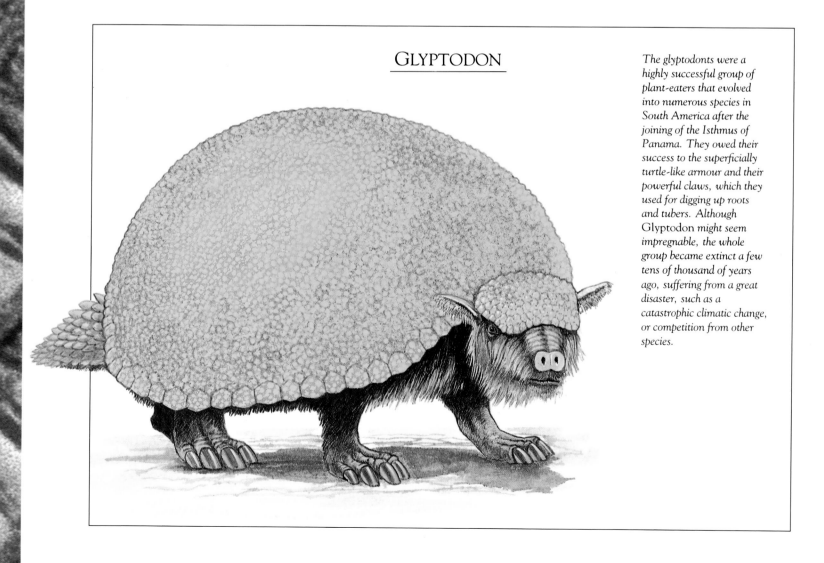

## GLYPTODON

*The glyptodonts were a highly successful group of plant-eaters that evolved into numerous species in South America after the joining of the Isthmus of Panama. They owed their success to the superficially turtle-like armour and their powerful claws, which they used for digging up roots and tubers. Although* Glyptodon *might seem impregnable, the whole group became extinct a few tens of thousand of years ago, suffering from a great disaster, such as a catastrophic climatic change, or competition from other species.*

# BEAVERS GREAT AND SMALL

Rodents – the gnawing mammals, with their perpetually growing front teeth – are the most diverse group of mammals in the world. They first appear in the fossil record in the late Paleocene epoch in North America, and by the Miocene they had blossomed into an incredible variety of genera and species that is still seen today from typical squirrels (among the most primitive of the order) to 120-pound/ 54.5-kilogram capybaras living in South America.

Among the most unusual of living rodents are the beavers, of which there are two species, European and American. Beavers are consummate engineers, building elaborate dams of sticks, limbs and tree trunks to block streams and small rivers. The large ponds that form behind the dam flood into surrounding woodland, giving the beavers access to the trees without going far from the security of the water.

Beavers, at up to 60 pounds/27 kilograms are among the largest of all rodents. They are equipped with huge incisor teeth for cutting; powered by massive jaw muscles, the teeth chew easily through wood, allowing the beaver to fell even large trees, which are then cut to length for building material and food (the inner bark is their preferred diet). Adaptations for an aquatic life include huge webbed hind feet, nostrils that can be closed with muscular flaps, waterproof fur and an ability to stay submerged for more than 15 minutes.

In the middle of the dam, the beavers build a conical lodge to house the colony, complete with underwater entrances and a roomy central chamber. Nearby is the winter larder, a tangled supply of green sticks jammed in the pond bottom that will be eaten when winter ice seals off the surface of the dam.

Beavers date to the Miocene epoch, but they have not always been aquatic. In what are now the American Plains, one genus, *Paleocastor*, pursued a subterranean life, digging corkscrewing burrows more than 8 feet/2.4 metres deep into the earth – burrows that filled in (as holes usually do) with soil of a different texture than the surrounding dirt. Such "fossil burrows" are common in many areas, including a few with fossilized *Paleocastor* bones entombed within.

**BELOW: The largest rodent in the Northern Hemisphere, the beaver can weigh as much as 60 pounds/27 kilograms,** subsisting on a diet of vegetation, especially water plants and the inner bark of various trees.

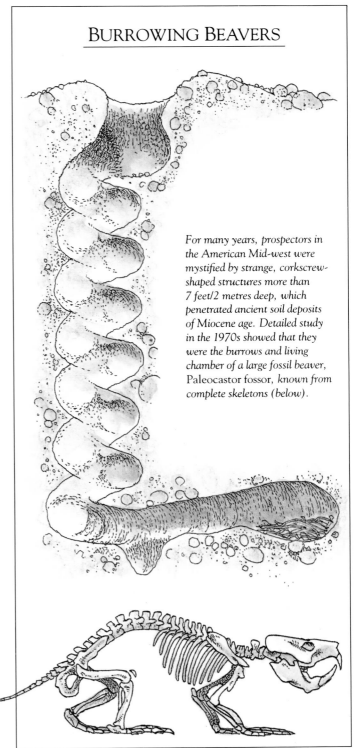

## BURROWING BEAVERS

*For many years, prospectors in the American Mid-west were mystified by strange, corkscrew-shaped structures more than 7 feet/2 metres deep, which penetrated ancient soil deposits of Miocene age. Detailed study in the 1970s showed that they were the burrows and living chamber of a large fossil beaver, Paleocastor fossor, known from complete skeletons (below).*

# WHALES

It may be that no other group of animals commands the awe and respect of the whales, which include the greatest creatures ever to roam the Earth. Modern cetaceans (the whales) are grouped into three super-families: the Platanistoidea, which includes the primitive river dolphins; the Delphinoidea, including the dolphins, porpoises and the beluga, narwhal and orca whales; and the Ziphiodea. This last contains, among others, the two best-known whale families, the Physeteridae, sperm whales, and the Balaenopteridae – the great baleen whales such as the blue and finback.

Watching a 70-foot/21-metre finback whale split the surface of the ocean with its smooth, wet back is enough to move even the most joyless soul, and at such times it is hard to imagine a terrestrial origin for the great whales. And yet the evidence showing their ancestors time on land is there, preserved in the fossil record.

Paleontologists trace the whales back to a group of land-dwelling mammals called mesonychids in the Paleocene. Although related to modern ungulates, the mesonychids appear to have been carnivorous, and the sea, with its rich selection of fish and molluscs, must have beckoned.

The oldest near-whale so far discovered is *Pakicetus*, which was rather small in comparison to modern cetaceans, and probably looked more like a sea lion than a cetacean, since it had functional hind limbs and could probably leave the water. It belonged to a group known as archaeocetes, which also contains the best-known prehistoric whale, *Basilosaurus*. Like *Pakicetus*, *Basilosaurus* had hind limbs, although by the

## THE EMPEROR LIZARD

In 1845, along the banks of the Tombigee River in Alabama in the United States, a self-educated fossil collector named Albert Koch excavated the first complete skeleton of a creature named from bone fragments as *Basilosaurus*, or "emperor lizard". The name seemed apt, for the bones showed a sea predator with fang-studded jaws and tremendous length – 114 feet/34.5 metres in the reconstruction that was produced by Koch.

Scientists of the day disparaged Koch's reconstruction, showing that at least three animals unwittingly contributed bones to the effort. Yet even they did not realize the biggest mistake of them all. *Basilosaurus* was not a dinosaur, as its name suggests, but a mammal. At a time when "sea serpent" reports were very much in the news, it was logical to assume Koch's find was a reptile, instead of the primitive whale it really was.

ABOVE: Its head encrusted with barnacled patches called callosities, a southern right whale drifts near a research boat off the Valdes Peninsula of Argentina.

# BASILOSAURUS

Basilosaurus was an early whale that bore an uncanny resemblance to a sea serpent, with its long, snake-like body and tiny head – in contrast to the bulky, thick-set body and large head of a modern whale. At lengths of 50–75 feet/15–23 metres, Basilosaurus was the largest mammal alive during its time. The rudimentary hind limbs, which no longer served any function, contained all the bones of fully-developed legs, but much reduced in size.

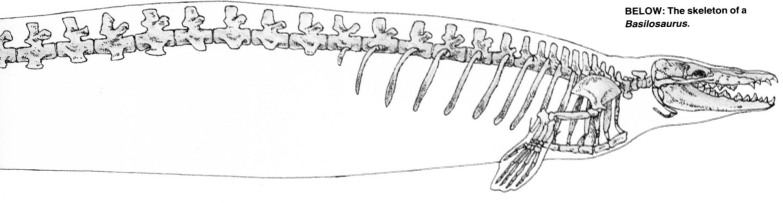

**BELOW: The skeleton of a Basilosaurus.**

Eocene, when this genus reached its heyday, the legs were tiny, useless vestiges. They did, however, contain all the bones found in the hind limbs of terrestrial mammals, a clear link to the creatures land-bound ancestors.

*Basilosaurus* was a huge animal, reaching lengths of 50 to 75 feet/15 to 23 metres, comparable to modern baleen whales. Its shape was far more serpentine, though, with a narrow head and long, rather thin body ending in small tail flukes; scientists speculate that *Basilosaurus* wriggled through a continuous series of S-curves in order to move, in contrast to modern cetaceans, which use strokes of their wide, powerful tail flukes to propel themselves forward.

Another difference lies in the teeth of the archaeocetes. Modern whales have two kinds of dentition – the simple, conical pegs of the toothed whales, and sheets of fibrous baleen, but no real teeth, in baleen whales. *Basilosaurus*, on the other hand, had 44 teeth of two kinds – large, fang-like teeth in the front of the jaw, and a set of cutting "molars" to the rear.

**BELOW: Tail flukes raised high, a right whale dives deep, an action the old whalers referred to as "sounding". Some ancient whales, like *Basilosaurus*, had much smaller flukes, and must have used serpentine body movements to swim.**

**RIGHT: Often called "the sea canary" because of its loud songs, the beluga whale is common in Arctic waters, sometimes travelling in herds of thousands during the calving season. Here a beluga whale swims near the sea bed.**

# BEARS

Rising on its hind legs to sniff for danger, a polar bear may stand more than 11 feet/3.3 metres tall and weigh in excess of 1,800 pounds/818 kilograms, making it the largest land carnivore in the world – an animal of immense power and speed, crafted by natural selection to fit the world of ice and ocean in which it lives. The polar bear may be the largest species today, but it seems that an extinct species may have been even bigger – the cave bear of the Pleistocene epoch, which was common in northern Eurasia during the ice ages.

Bears are members of the order Carnivora, the large group of meat-eaters that also includes the cats, dogs, weasels and procyonids such as raccoons. But more so than any other group of carnivores, bears have followed their own evolutionary path. Not long after the earliest carnivores split into two major groups in the late Eocene epoch, the feliforms and the caniforms, the immediate ancestors of the bears evolved, a group known as amphiocyonids, or bear-dogs. Named for their canine bodies and heavy, bear-like skulls, the amphiocyonids survived until the Pliocene.

Modern bears are carnivores with a strongly omnivorous diet; there is almost nothing a bear will not eat, or at least attempt to eat. Grizzly bears will attack and kill elk, bison and deer, but feed more often on carrion – and most often of all on grasses, tubers, berries and nuts. North America's most common bear, the black bear, depends mostly on fruits, berries and forest food such as acorns and beechnuts, and there is evidence that the giant cave bear was entirely vegetarian.

The polar bear of the Arctic is the most consistently carnivorous of the family, preying heavily on seals captured at their breathing holes, as well as seeking out beached whale or walrus carcasses. Yet even polar bears switch to a diet heavy in vegetable matter during the brief northern summer.

**ABOVE: The largest land carnivore in the world, the polar bear stalks seals along the Arctic coast and icepack.**

**BELOW: The black bear is North America's most common bear,** found from Florida to California and north to Canada and Alaska. Not all are black; many, especially in the west, are chocolate or cinnamon, while a few coastal forms may even be bluish-white.

# THE CATS

Among the earliest well-defined groups of carnivores were the felines, which first appear in Oligocene fossil beds, and probably evolved late in the Eocene. Today, the family Felidae is found on every continent except Australia and Antarctica, with 37 species ranging from wild cats scarcely larger than house tabbies, to Siberian tigers, the world's largest cat, now reduced to a few hundred individuals in the boreal forests of northern Asia.

Wild felines have shown an amazing adaptability to varying climates and habitats. The mountain lion of the Western Hemisphere, for example, was once found over virtually all of North America, from British Columbia to New England and Florida; it is also at home in the arid mountains of Mexico, the rain forests of Central America and the Amazon basin, the grassy pampas of Argentina and the rugged, snowcapped peaks of Patagonia. This most adaptable of the world's cats is also known by a host of names: puma, cougar, catamount and panther are just a few.

Many areas have a dominant species of big cat – the mountain lion in North America, the jaguar in New World jungles, the lion in Africa (and previously in Greece, Turkey and the Middle East) and the tiger in Asia. Fossils from the Pleistocene turn this list on its head, however, with tigers once having also been found in Africa, and large cave lions living in Europe and North America.

Most modern cats are solitary, but African lions, and the critically endangered Asian lion of India, are social, living in prides of related females and cubs, with a dominant male at the top of the family unit. The females do most of the hunting, but the male will always eat first – the proverbial "lion's share". Recent observations with night-vision equipment has shown that lions may scavenge the kills of hyenas more than previously thought, although they are capable predators in their own right.

The most unusual of the living cats is the cheetah, which has given up the rectractable claws of the other felines for the long limbs and greyhound-shape of a runner. Indeed, cheetahs have been clocked at more than 60 miles per hour/96 kilometres per hour, making them the fastest mammal in the world. Today just one species survives, but during the Pleistocene as many as 11 cheetah species could be found in both the Old and New Worlds.

**BELOW: Most cats are solitary, but African lions have developed a sophisticated social structure. Here, a magnificently maned male watches while females and cubs feed on an antelope that has been hunted down.**

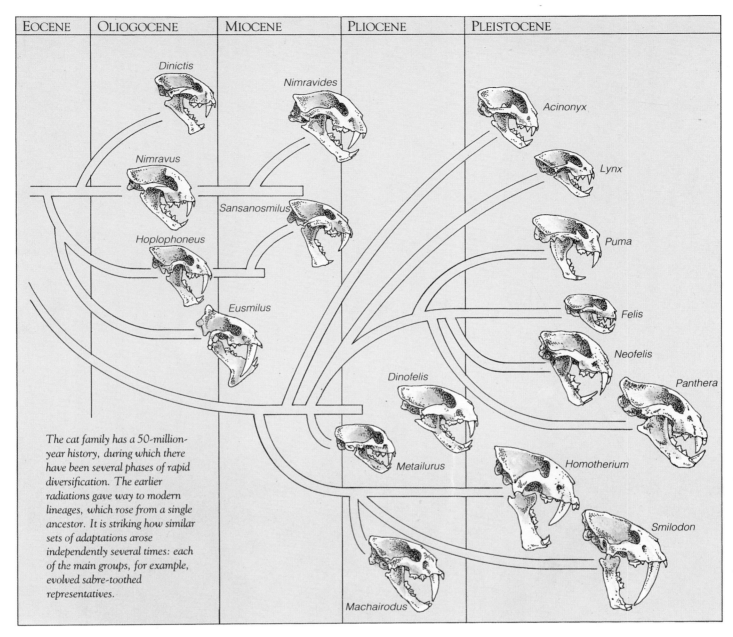

| EOCENE | OLIOGOCENE | MIOCENE | PLIOCENE | PLEISTOCENE |
|---|---|---|---|---|

*Dinictis*

*Nimravides*

*Acinonyx*

*Nimravus*

*Lynx*

*Sansanosmilus*

*Puma*

*Hoplophoneus*

*Felis*

*Eusmilus*

*Neofelis*

*Dinofelis*

*Panthera*

The cat family has a 50-million-year history, during which there have been several phases of rapid diversification. The earlier radiations gave way to modern lineages, which rose from a single ancestor. It is striking how similar sets of adaptations arose independently several times: each of the main groups, for example, evolved sabre-toothed representatives.

*Metailurus*

*Homotherium*

*Smilodon*

*Machairodus*

**LEFT: The mountain lion, known by a host of names, is found in a host of places – from the northern Rockies south to Patagonia, and in habitats that range from desert to rain forest.**

# SABRE-TOOTHED NIGHTMARES

One of the most striking features of feline evolution is the repeated development of "sabre-toothed tigers", as the cats with extraordinarily long canine teeth are commonly known.

Although sabre-toothed cats first appeared in the Oligocene, by far the most famous sabre-tooth is *Smilodon*, found during the Pleistocene in North America and Europe; its skeletons have been recovered in fair quantity from ancient tar seeps like the one at La Brea, California. Its canine teeth are remarkable – more than 6 inches/15 centimetres long and curved like scimitars, they are even flattened, side-to-side, instead of being round like most cat canines.

*Smilodon*'s presence in the tar pits (where trapped animals attracted such confirmed scavengers as teratorn condors), as well as doubt over the effectiveness of such outsized teeth for hunting, led many scientists to conclude that *Smilodon* and the other sabre-tooths may well have been carrion eaters; a high incidence of bone disease scarring on their skeletons (common among scavengers) seemed to support this theory. Today, however, paleontologists are returning to the belief that sabre-tooths hunted and killed their prey, although the gigantic fangs are now thought to have been used largely to cut meat, rather than kill it.

Cats were not the only mammalian sabre-tooths. In another of the many parallels between marsupial and placental evolution, *Thylacosmilus* and its relatives evolved in South America during the Pleistocene, echoing *Smilodon* to the north. Both variations on the theme died out with the extinction of the large grazing mammals, on which both presumably relied for food.

## SABRE TEETH

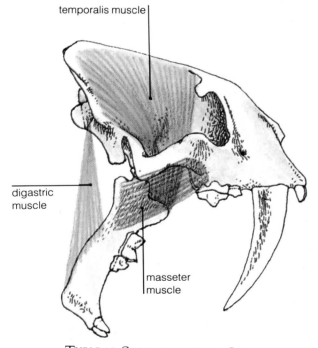

TYPICAL SABRE-TOOTHED CAT

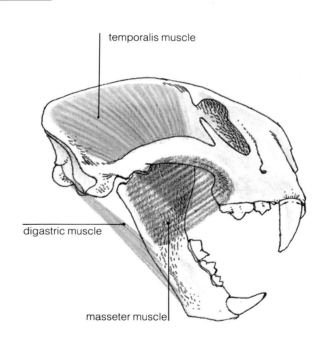

TYPICAL MODERN CAT

*The sabre-toothed type of cat skull involves major changes in the shape and mobility of the lower jaw, as well as in the size of the canine teeth. The jaw action was highly specialized compared to more typical cats. A modern cat uses its canine teeth for stabbing at prey, its incisors for nipping off flesh, and its cheek teeth for tearing tough flesh and cutting gristle and bone. In sabre-tooths, the main jaw movement was the "pincer-stab", when the canines were pushed or stabbed into the flesh of the prey and the jaws closed to lever off a chunk of flesh. The masseter muscle could relax and allow the lower jaw to drop, so that the sabre-toothed cat had an enormous gape.*

## PARALLEL EVOLUTION OF SABRE-TOOTHED "CATS"

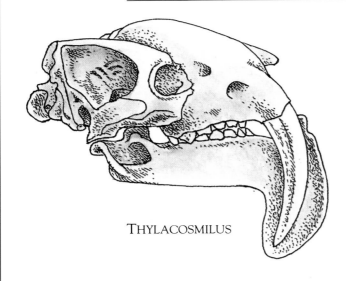

THYLACOSMILUS

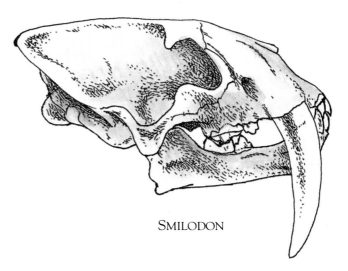

SMILODON

Marsupial and placental mammals show many instances of parallel evolution, including marsupial versions of cats, dogs, moles, shrews, squirrels and others. A good example is the development of the marsupial sabre-tooth Thylacosmilus, the equivalent of the placental sabre-toothed cats, such as Smilodon.

## THYLACOSMILUS

The marsupial sabre-tooth Thylacosmilus *was one of numerous sabre-toothed carnivores that evolved. It had the longest sabre teeth of any of these animals, being 8 inches/20 centimetres in length. In addition, and uniquely among sabre-tooths, the long teeth grew continuously, to compensate for wear at the tips.*

# WILD DOG TO HOUSE DOG

There is scarcely a corner of the world without a wild canine of one sort or another; in fact, only Antarctica, the Greenland icepack and a few large islands like Madagascar are lacking a native species.

The most widespread of this far-ranging family is the grey wolf, *Canis lupus*, with species, subspecies and races once found over virtually all of the Northern Hemisphere and beyond – in fact, it has the widest natural range of any land mammal with the exception of man. More so than many other wild canines, the wolf is a social animal, living in rigidly structured packs and hunting co-operatively.

Such co-operation and instinctive need for companionship made the wolf a natural target for early domestication by humans, and it was undoubtedly the first such animal brought out of the wild, perhaps as long as 20,000 years ago. While many specialists believe wolves were first domesticated in the Near East, others claim the small Chinese or Indian wolves to be the true ancestors of the dog.

Since then, domestic dogs have been selectively bred for shape, size and colour, so that today a huge variety of breeds exists, from giant mastiffs to tiny terriers. It is hard to credit that all are the same species, *Canis familiaris*.

When allowed to interbreed freely, the carefully selected characteristics of the purebreeds disappear, and the resulting mongrels are often so strikingly similar – short, solidly coloured coat, long upcurled tail, erect ears – that some believe this to be a genetic echo of the first domestic dogs. Australian dingos fit this description, and although they roam wild, it seems likely they arrived in Australia in a semidomestic state along with Aborigine hunters.

Biologists usually group wolves, coyotes, dogs and jackals (all of which readily hybridize) in one group, while the many species of fox are placed together. Foxes tend to have shorter legs, longer tails and an overall smaller size, and they usually hunt alone or in pairs, rather than forming packs. Not every canine, however, fits into a neat category. The hunting dog of Africa – one of that continent's most misunderstood and beleaguered predators – is unique in many respects, as are the maned wolf and two species of strange rain-forest dogs from South America.

## HOUSE CATS: JOHNNY-COME-LATELIES

While fossil evidence indicates that dogs were domesticated as much as 20,000 years ago, cats have been human companions for a far briefer time, perhaps as little as 3,600 years. It seems certain they were first domesticated in the Mediterranean basin, possibly in Egypt, where cats were worshiped as incarnations of the gods.

The domestic cat's direct ancestor is the wild cat, *Felis silvestris*, which is still found throughout much of Africa, the Middle East, Scotland and parts of central and southern Europe. Wild cats are almost indistinguishable from large grey tabbies, but the tail is heavier and banded, and the coat is lightly striped rather than blotched.

ABOVE: A close, and threatened, relative of the grey fox, the diminutive kit fox is adapted to life in the hot, arid southwest United States; its large ears, for example, aid in heat dispersal.

LEFT: Backlit by the low winter sun, a grey wolf pauses in the Montana woods. Grey wolves have the widest natural range of any mammal save man, covering most of the Northern Hemisphere.

# SEALS, SEA LIONS AND THEIR RELATIVES

Those with only a hazy notion of mammalian evolution often make the mistake of assuming that the pinnipeds ("finned foot") – seals, sea lions, fur seals and walruses – must be some imperfect step between land animals and whales. Like most assumptions based on appearances, it is wrong.

Life in water makes certain, immutable demands on any creature, be it fish, bird, reptile or mammal. The high resistance of water, for example, leads to streamlining, and since a broad pushing surface is best for propulsion, it is no surprise that the flukes of whales, webbed feet of ducks and flippers of seals should be the result. Still, there are differences. True, or earless, seals have so thoroughly cut their ties to land that they must inch forward on their bellies like grubs when they haul themselves out of the water. Sea lions and fur seals, in contrast, can turn their hind flippers forward and use them to walk in a semi-upright position; they also retain small, external ears, and scientists believe their ancestors did not return to the sea as early as did the earless seals.

Pinnipeds are adapted to life in cold water internally as well as externally. Most remarkable is their ability to dive to extreme depths, and for long periods of time; a Weddell seal in Antarctica spent almost an hour submerged, diving to more than 1,800 feet/545 metres. Fatty blubber insulates the seal's body, while a physiological reaction known as the mammalian diving reflex slows the heartbeat and metabolism when the animal submerges. A similar reflex has been known to occur in humans that fall into cold water, resulting in "drowning" victims that miraculously recover from long periods underwater.

Fossils indicate that pinnipeds are descended from an early branch of the carnivores, dating to the late Eocene. One of the best-known seal lion ancestors is *Enaliarctos*, an otter-sized fish-hunter of the early Miocene that would have looked very much like a modern pinniped, with a short tail and wide flippers on all four legs. The hind limbs were still quite robust, however.

Walruses have long posed something of a puzzle as to their ancestry, since they display the lack of external ear cartilage found in true seals, but have the same sort of forward-rotating hind flippers as fur seals and sea lions. Paleontologists now believe that walruses are more closely related to true seals, from which they diverged about 15 million years ago.

**LEFT: A bristled snout and long tusks help the walrus in gathering its favourite food – shellfish, siphoned off the bottom of cold Arctic waters.**

**RIGHT: Hauled out on a rock at low tide, a harbour seal enjoys basking in the sunshine, while the safety of the water is only a quick dive away.**

## EARLY MARINE MAMMALS

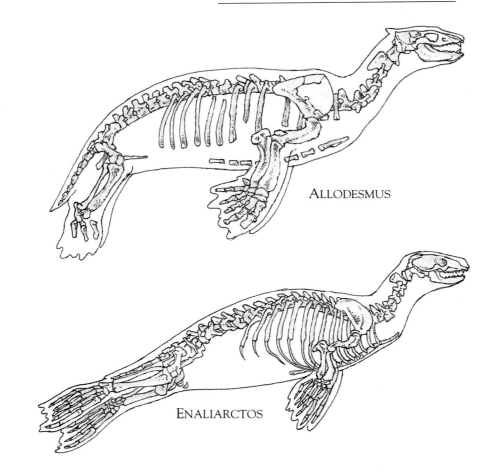

ALLODESMUS

ENALIARCTOS

Allodesmus *from the Pacific coast of the United States, although superficially like a sealion, in fact belonged to another, now extinct group, the desmatophocids. These had large eyes and primitive ears, while modern sealions have tiny eyes and ears specialized for underwater hunting.* Enaliarctos, *again discovered on the Pacific coast of the United States, appears to be close to the ancestry of modern sealions, even though it may have had a considerably more terrestrial lifestyle.*

# HOOFED MAMMALS

The sprawling group known as hoofed mammals may be Mammalia's finest flowering, containing many of the most graceful and beautiful members of the class.

Known collectively as ungulates (from the Latin word *ungula*, hoof), they are lumped in two broad divisions – the odd-toed ungulates, including horses, tapirs and rhinos; and the even-toed ungulates, a larger group including deer, cattle, pigs, hippos, camels, giraffes and others.

Few people think of hooves as toes, and yet they are, and much of the ungulates' evolutionary history is a tale of the steady loss of toes, especially among horses – from four in the earliest horse ancestors to one in the modern species. The first protoungulates appear in the fossil record in the Paleocene epoch, a group known as condylarths, which many paleontologists now believe were not a true order but a collection of similar, but unrelated, hoofed mammals.

By the Eocene, ungulate evolution had taken a strange twist: they became meat-eaters. The mesonychids were carnivorous ungulates, many the size of modern coyotes, but some eclipsing today's brown bears for size and weight. The true ungulates in the modern sense arose in the Eocene as well. The perissodactyls, as odd-toed ungulates are properly known, came to the fore then, and exploded into adaptive vigour in the Miocene and Pliocene epochs; artiodactyls, or even-toed ungulates, followed suit on a slightly delayed scale, but flowered at roughly the same time.

Evolutionarily, the ungulates' fortunes have waned somewhat since then. The mass extinctions of the Pleistocene epoch greatly reduced many once-important families, such as camels and horses, although ungulates remain the most important herbivorous mammals on Earth.

**BELOW: From their beginnings in the Eocene epoch, the hoofed mammals, known as ungulates, have split into two major lineages – odd-toed ungulates like zebras, tapirs and rhinos, and even-toed ungulates like deer, hippos and pronghorns.**

# HORSES

No other group of ungulates have been tracked so closely through their evolutionary history as the horses; in fact, *"Eohippus"*, the dawn horse, now known as *Hyracotherium*, is one of the few extinct mammals many people can name. The story begins in North America during the Eocene, with the appearance of *Hyracotherium*, a four-toed animal the size of a small dog; at first glance, it scarcely seems horse-like, although the long legs and cylindrical head were already evident. Over the course of millions of years, horses underwent a radical reduction in the number of toes, eventually producing a strong, sturdy leg perfect for running. By the Oligocene, *Mesohippus* was down to three digits, a large central toe with two smaller spurs for side support. *Merychippus* ran across the plains of the Miocene on hooves with vestigial dewclaws on either side,

## THE QUAGGA

When Europeans first arrived in southern Africa, they found a peculiar variety of zebra, striped on the front half of the body but plain brown elsewhere, with a white tail and legs. It did not yip like other zebras, but barked; the call sounded to them like *quagga!* and that's what they named the beast.

The quagga did not last, however. They were systematically wiped out, and by 1883 the only things remaining were two dozen mounted specimens. Modern biochemical analysis of the DNA in the preserved skins showed the quagga to be a closely related subspecies of the surviving Burchell's zebra, so game ranchers are hoping to selectively breed Burchell's with faint stripes to produce a "near-quagga" that would, at least, look like the lost animal. Regardless of looks, however, the true quagga is a species gone for good.

**BELOW: Grevy's zebra is a larger, more finely striped horse than the common Grant's, or Burchell's, zebra. Regardless of species, however, zebras have proven a far more difficult animal to domesticate than their northern cousin the wild horse.**

**RIGHT: Descended from the stocky, stiff-maned wild horses of the Eurasian plains, the domestic horse has now completely supplanted the original wild strain, which is extinct with the exception of a few captive herds.**

# HORSE EVOLUTION

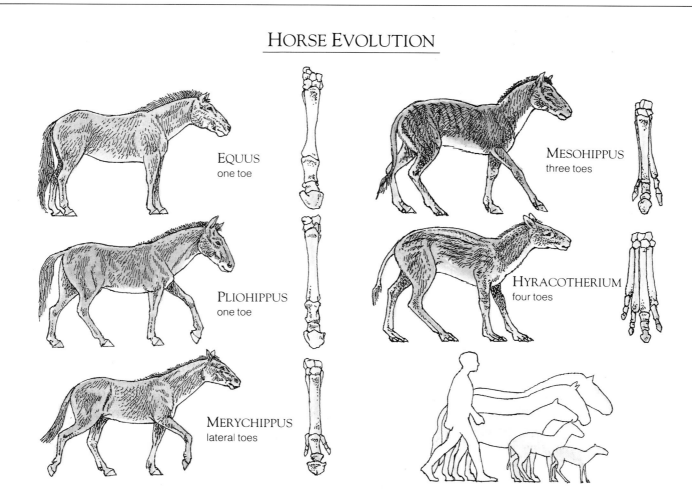

EQUUS
one toe

MESOHIPPUS
three toes

PLIOHIPPUS
one toe

HYRACOTHERIUM
four toes

MERYCHIPPUS
lateral toes

*The evolution of the horse is often used to show how a single lineage progresses along one path through time. In the story, the small Eocene ancestor Hyracotherium was a dog-sized animal that lived in North America and Europe. It had four toes on each foot, and browsed in lush forests. During the*

*Oligocene and Miocene, horses such as Mesohippus and Merychippus evolved rapidly in North America, to exploit the spreading dry grasslands. They became larger (see the scale drawing), lost toes, and acquired deeper teeth for chewing the tougher grasses. Adaptation to life on the open*

*plains led to larger body size and less of the side toes, as in Pliohippus and the modern horse Equus. However, we now know that the story is not quite so simple, and that there were many branchings of the evolutionary pathway and extinctions of species along the rather complex way.*

which vanished completely by the late Miocene and early Pliocene. This period of time also saw the appearance of *Pliohippus* in North America and modern horses of the genus *Equus* in the Old World.

Horses reached a zenith during the Miocene, a time of unprecedented expansion that included *Hipparion*, one of the most successful horse genera ever. From their original base in North America, horses fanned out into Eurasia, Africa and, once the Central American land bridge formed, to South America. Most of these Miocene horses became extinct by the early Pliocene, with modern *Equus* horses replacing them in most regions. In one of the strangest twists of evolutionary fate, North America's wild horses died out late in the Pleistocene, and by historical times only eight species of horses, including zebras, the wild ass and Przewalski's horse, remained – all in Africa, the Middle East and Asia. The "wild" horses of the western United States are actually feral escapees and their offspring.

## WILD HORSES

Cave paintings and fossil remains show that wild horses were, until the end of the Pleistocene, fairly common in Europe and Asia. But sometime between the fall of the Paleolithic cultures and the rise of Western civilization, these wild horses disappeared from most of their former haunts, even while their newly domesticated descendants were flourishing under human care. The last herds of truly wild horses were found in the 1870s in Mongolia, and are named after their discoverer, Nikolai Przewalski.

Today, Przewalski's horse, with its brown coat and short, stiff mane, is probably extinct in the wild, but captive herds are carefully managed to ensure maximum genetic diversity. Several other wild equids are also in serious danger of becoming extinct, among them the African and Indian wild asses and two varieties of zebra, the Grevy's and the Cape Mountain zebra.

# TAPIRS

Appearing suddenly from the gloom of the rain forest, with its huge body and pendulous snout, a tapir looks more like a tiny elephant than a relative of the horse. Yet – snout aside – tapirs are very close to what the ancestral horse looked like, a freeze-frame of evolutionary history, right down to the four toes on the front foot and three on the hind.

There are only four species of tapirs, three of them in the New World tropics and one in Malaysia. Until the Pleistocene, tapirs were also found in North America and Europe, but the drastic cooling trend brought on by the onset of the ice ages wiped them out in all but the warmest regions.

Tapirs are big-bodied herbivores, weighing up to 600 pounds/273 kilograms, a bulk they sustain by browsing constantly on leaves and fruit. Often found near rivers, tapirs swim easily and occasionally even sleep in water (the snout may play a role as a snorkel), but they do not hesitate to wander great distances inland as well. They are nearly hairless, except for a stiff mane between the ears of the New World species. New World tapirs are black or brown, but the Asian tapir has a large area of white in the back and flanks. Known as "mountain cows" in some parts of Central America, tapirs have been heavily hunted in many areas, and wherever they are found, they are shy, nocturnal creatures.

**BELOW: An early tapir from the Eocene period. It lived in a warm, humid environment among rich vegetation, much as do its modern descendants.**

**RIGHT: Looking much like its own early ancestors and the ancestors of the modern horse, the Baird's tapir is common in Central America.**

# RHINOS, WOOLLY AND OTHERWISE

Imagine an animal somewhat akin in shape to a giraffe, standing more than 17 feet/5 metres tall, not slender and lithe but hugely muscular and ponderous. This behemoth was *Indricotherium*, an Oligocene monster rhinoceros once known as *Baluchitherium*, and the largest land mammal ever to have roamed the Earth. Found in Asia, it probably weighed as much as four or five modern African elephants. For all its size, or perhaps because of its size, *Indricotherium* had no horn on its head; it probably needed nothing but its enormous bulk for defence against predators.

Rhino evolution apparently began during the Eocene epoch in North America. The first rhinos bore little resemblance to the tank-like creatures of today; they were small and lightly built for running, four-toed and hornless. That changed during the Miocene and Pliocene, when rhinos increased in size, developing shorter, sturdier legs and their famous facial

"horns" – actually specialized bundles of dermal fibres fused together into a rock-like mass.

In subsequent epochs their diversity declined. The most notable of the more recent rhinos were the Pleistocene's woolly rhinoceros of Europe, *Coelodonta*, and the even larger *Elasmotherium*, which had a single, head-filling horn of epic proportions. As with other ice age mammals, we know a little about the woolly rhino's colour (reddish brown) not only from cave art, but also from actual specimens that have been found preserved in oil seeps.

Today there are five surviving rhino species, two in Africa (the two-horned white and the one-horned black) and three in Asia (the Sumatran, Javan and great Indian). All five are endangered by poaching and habitat destruction, particularly the black rhino, the horn of which is especially coveted for high-priced knife handles in the Middle East.

## BRONTOTHERIUM

*The brontotheres, or titanotheres, were abundant in the early Tertiary of North America and eastern Asia. Brontotherium itself stood 8 feet/2.5 metres tall at the shoulder. Although the*

*Brontotheres looked very like rhinos, the animals are not at all closely related. They are a good example of how evolution produces similar animals to fill similar ecological niches.*

ABOVE: Oxpeckers look in the folds of a black rhino's hide. Among the most critically endangered of Africa's animals, the black rhino has been relentlessly poached for its horns.

## THE LARGEST LAND ANIMALS

The early rhinoceros *Indricotherium*, with its astonishing 32-ton(ne) bulk, was for years the largest creature considered to be completely terrestrial. Admittedly, the great sauropod dinosaurs were much larger, but traditional thought held them to be swamp dwellers, trapped in an aquatic lifestyle by the need to have their massive bodies supported party by water. Scientists were convinced that the giant rhino was about as big as a fully terrestrial animal could become. However, just as the discovery of giant pterosaurs forced a rethinking on maximum flight sizes, recent advances in dinosaur paleontology have exploded the belief about maximum terrestrial sizes. The sauropods have, in effect, been released from the swamps. *Ultrasaurus*, 150 feet/45 metres long may have weighed 150 ton(ne)s, four and a half times the mass of *Indricotherium*, but we now know that it walked freely about the land.

BELOW: The massive *Indricotheum* browsed on larger vegetation in Asia during the Oligocene.

# WILD BOARS AND MONSTER HOGS

Confined to the Old World, the true pigs of the family Suidae date back some 50 million years. Among their earliest ancestors were the oreodonts, a group of small four-toed grazers also considered ancestral to camels, which lived in the Oligocene and early Miocene epochs.

Today there are eight species of living pigs, including the Eurasian wild boar, from which the domestic pig is descended; in fact, escaped pigs tend to revert to the typical boar form – dark coat, large head, compact hindquarters – after just several generations in the wild. Other species of wild pigs include the warthog and forest hog of Africa and the long-tusked babirusa of Indonesia.

The pigs had their own giant ancestors, most notably *Afrochoerus*, which was the size of a rhino with four tusks curving almost straight out from the front of the mouth. Its size is reminiscent of *Dinohyus*, a giant hog of the American Miocene now considered only distantly related to true pigs.

Pigs are considered the most primitive of the surviving artiodactyls, with a generalized diet that includes almost anything they can find – plants, fruit, small animals, insects and carrion. Unlike the other main artiodactyl branch, pigs are not ruminants – that is, they do not possess multichambered stomachs or chew a cud.

While superficially similar, the New World peccaries of the family Tayassuidae split from the main branch of pig evolution early on. Among other differences, peccaries have fewer teeth, fused leg bones and young that can follow the mother from birth, instead of spending their first days in a nest, as is the case with the true pigs.

ABOVE: The African warthog would win no beauty contests, with its flaring tusks and grizzled fur, but it is one of the more successful of the world's wild pigs.

LEFT: Superficially similar to true pigs, the peccaries of the New World actually belong to a separate family, the Tayassuidae. This is a female collared peccary, the most common species, and her young.

# ANTLERED WONDERS: DEER AND THEIR ALLIES

The cold, acidic peat bogs of northern Europe have, on occasion, offered up one of the fossil jewels of the ice age – the skull and antlers of the Irish elk, *Megaloceros*, which sported the largest rack of antlers on any deer at any time. The antlers are staggeringly big, sweeping back and out for a spread of more than 11 feet/3.3 metres, twice the size of the biggest North American elk today.

From the tiny spikes of the Chinese tufted deer to the vast racks of moose and caribou, the deer are known for their antlers, the extravagance of bone that grows from the head of the male (and, in the case of the caribou and reindeer, also the female). Antlers are solid bone, unlike the horn sheaths of cattle and sheep, and also unlike true horns they are shed at the end of the mating season and a new rack grown again the next spring; new antlers are the fastest-growing structure in any animal, expanding by a quarter-inch (half-centimetre) a day. Biologists estimate a male deer invests as much energy into growing antlers as a female will into raising her young. Why go to such trouble for an ornament that isn't even permanent?

Possessing a large rack, research has shown, helps tremendously in mating with the largest number of females and dominating smaller males. Such "secondary sex characteristics" as antlers, large horns, dazzling colours or other adornments catch the eye of potential mates and frighten rivals – and because such characteristics are a physical drain on their owners, those that can succeed despite them are probably genetically fitter than those without.

Cervids (as deer are technically known) rose to prominence during the Miocene, when a dry climate worldwide promoted the spread of grasslands. Nor was *Megaloceros* the only dramatically antlered species; extinct cervids included genera with antlers sprouting in thick, multipronged bushes, like the bizarre *Eucladoceros*, and *Hoplitomeryx* which had as many as five horn-shaped antlers and protruding, fang-like canine teeth.

**BELOW: Originally an Old World species, the elk (known as red deer in Europe) spread to North America via the Bering land bridge. Although Rocky** **Mountain elk are now restricted to remoter mountains, they evolved as a grassland species, and once thrived on the great plains of North America.**

## HORNS AND ANTLERS

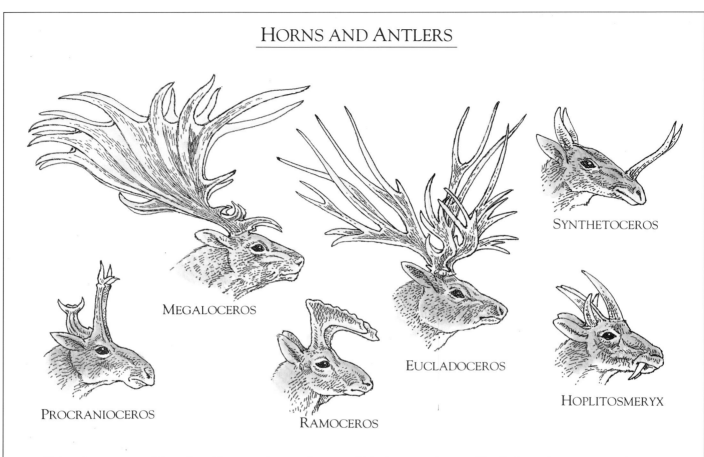

MEGALOCEROS

SYNTHETOCEROS

PROCRANIOCEROS

RAMOCEROS

EUCLADOCEROS

HOPLITOSMERYX

Today, the most successful ungulates (that is, large herbivorous mammals) are the horned, even-toed artiodactyls, such as deer, antelope, cattle and giraffes. The term "horn" includes a great range of shapes and types, and it is almost certain that horns evolved independently four of five times. Only cattle and antelope have true horns, consisting of a bony core and a horny sheath, neither of which are shed. Giraffes have a bony core covered with skin, while deer have antlers which are shed annually. The creatures shown here are all extinct species of deer, except for Ramoceros and Synthetoceros.

**LEFT The North American moose is the largest surviving member of the deer family, with some bulls standing 7 feet/2 metres at the shoulder and weighing 1,800 pounds/ 818 kilograms.**

# ANCIENT OXEN AND DOMESTIC COWS

The Paleolithic hunters of Europe left a precious record of their world on the walls of caves – magnificent paintings of wild animals, from deer and woolly rhinos to cave lions and horses. By far the most dramatic depictions, however, are those of wild oxen, like the gigantic black bulls that rampage across the rock of Lascaux, a cave in France. This marvellous creature was the aurochs, the great ox of Europe, and the ancestor of today's modern cattle.

A bull aurochs weighed more than a ton(ne), and was jet black with a white muzzle and a white stripe down the spine; African aurochs (to judge from cave paintings) were rusty brown instead. The horns were sweeping and wide, no doubt a deadly defence against brown bears and wolves.

The aurochs lasted much longer than the rest of Europe's large mammals, and only died out in 1627 after centuries of overhunting. That its genes are still present in modern cattle, despite 9,000 years of domestication, was clearly shown when scientists selectively bred a "near-aurochs" that looked much like the ancestral species.

Cattle are but one facet of the diverse family Bovidae, which also includes bison, true antelopes, sheep and goats. While quite different on the surface, virtually all have permanent horns with bone cores, which are carried by females as well as males; they have vestigial dewclaws or none at all; and all are ruminants.

**BELOW: Although a fairly modern breed, the highland cow has a hint of the aurochs in its looks – the sweeping horns, the heavy build.**

**BOTTOM: Bison are but one branch of the diverse family Bovidae, which includes animals such as cattle, sheep, goats and muskoxen.**

**OVERLEAF: Southern Europe in the late Miocene, a time when the climate was subtropical and the fauna looked, in modern terms, in some ways faintly "African".**

Machairodus

Amphicyon

Deinotherium

Ramapithecus

Samotherium

Gomphotherium

Hipparion

# THE ENIGMATIC PRONGHORN

In a flat-out run, moving like an ochre blur against the prairie grass, a pronghorn can hit 60 miles per hour (96 kilometres per hour). It can easily outdistance even the fastest of its predators.

Extreme speed is but one of the many fascinating things about the pronghorn, the lone member of the family Antilocapridae. Once there were many more, however; in the Miocene and later, as many as 40 genera existed, some with truly bizarre horn shapes. Today's pronghorn sports forked horns that curl back over the buck's head, but ancient pronghorns had horns that spiralled, flattened into shovels or looked like a child's catapult.

Pronghorns are lovely animals. The sexes are similar in colour – yellow-brown, with white rump, sides and neck markings – and most does have horns, although not as large as the buck's. The tail is a tiny stub surrounded by a white rosette of hair, which the pronghorn can flash erect when alarmed, a visual signal that can be seen for miles across the prairie.

One traditional theory holds that, in the absence of bison in North America during the Miocene, antilocaprids spread out into most of the plains grazing niches. The arrival of long-horned and other bison during the Pleistocene may have doomed the family's pre-eminence, although the sole surviving species still numbered in the tens of millions when white settlers began carving up the plains for cattle. Today, about 750,000 pronghorns inhabit western North America.

A pronghorn can sprint almost twice as fast as a coyote, its most common predator, but scientists think its speed originally evolved as a defence against a completely different adversary – cheetahs, which were found until the Pleistocene in North America. With the great extinction the cheetahs vanished, but the pronghorns remained, still racing under the wide sky.

**BELOW: Three pronghorn does race across the prairie, capable of speeds of 60 mph/96 km/h – speed perhaps evolved as a defence against now-extinct New World cheetahs.**

# OTHER EVEN-TOED UNGULATES

The lineage of artiodactyls is an endlessly varied one, encompassing not just the deer, pigs, bovids and pronghorns, but a variety of other plant-eaters, including the camels, giraffes and hippos – creatures of dissimilar shape, united by the number of toes they possess.

Hippos are usually considered primitive ungulates allied with the pigs. As with so many mammals, hippos were more common, widespread and diverse in the past than today, when there are only two surviving species, including a diminutive pygmy hippo from western Africa. Dwarf hippos were also found during the Pleistocene epoch on a number of Mediterranean islands, part of a unique pygmy fauna there.

The remaining artiodactyls are grouped with the higher ruminants. Camels and their relatives, the New World llama, vicuña and guanaco, first evolved in North America during the Eocene, eventually spreading over much of the world. Ironically they, like the horse, became extinct in their native land during the Pleistocene, although camels remain today in South America and Asia. A 19th-century U.S. Army experiment to use Asian camels in the southwest of the United States might well have worked (the camels ate many desert plants other grazers scorned), but ranchers shot the humped beasts and the plan was abandoned.

**BELOW: An African hippo shows its deadly tusks – which are one reason why this species is considered one of the most dangerous big game animals in Africa.**

**BOTTOM: The tiny pygmy hippo from western Africa is considerably smaller than its better-known cousin; other dwarf hippos evolved on a number of Mediterranean islands, but have since become extinct.**

Camels showed an early evolutionary trend towards long legs and necks, but no other group of mammals has taken that path to the degree shown by giraffes. Short-necked giraffes were standard for millions of years, dating back to the Miocene epoch; in fact in the case of the modern forest okapi, a short neck is still standard. These were animals like *Libytherium* from the African Pleistocene, which had peculiar horns that curved back over the head, in contrast to the tiny, skin-covered bumps on modern giraffes. Interestingly, the neck lengthened through time, not by the addition of vertebrae, but through elongation of existing bones. Like most mammals, a giraffe has only seven neck bones.

**BELOW: Giraffes have the most elongated necks of any mammal, but the stretch did not involve adding vertebrae; the neck bones themselves lengthened.**

# ELEPHANTS, MAMMOTHS AND MASTODONTS

The African elephant is the largest land animal alive today, and both it and its smaller Asian cousin are the last survivors of a remarkable order, the Proboscidae.

As every child knows, an elephant's most characteristic feature is its trunk, the greatly elongated snout that serves as a fifth limb; the tip of the trunk is so dexterous that it can pick up a coin. And although an elephant can hold and squirt water from its trunk, it cannot drink or eat through it.

Paleontologists trace elephants back to the Old World Eocene epoch. *Moeritherium*, the best-known of the early proboscids, may have looked like a cross between a large pig and a small hippo; unlike later elephants it had no trunk, and it had six large teeth on either side of the upper jaw, compared to just one each side in modern elephants. *Moeritherium* also lacked tusks, although its incisor teeth (which later evolved into tusks) were already the size of large fangs.

The Oligocene and Miocene epochs marked the first great dispersal of elephants. Size increased dramatically from the

### FROZEN ANIMALS

The true woolly mammoth, *Mammuthus primigenius*, is all but unique among fossil species, for its remains have been found frozen in permafrost soil in Alaska and Siberia, giving scientists a remarkable look at its woolly coat and even its stomach contents. Only a handful of other ice age mammals, including bison, have been found in this condition, which probably resulted from landslides along the edges of Arctic rivers. Buried in the sudden fall of soil, the animals were quickly frozen and so perfectly preserved that Russian scientists found the meat edible – the first known example of deep frozen food!

**BELOW: With the babies safely in sight, a herd of African elephants marches across the East African savannah under the guidance of an old cow. A** recent worldwide ban on ivory imports has helped slow the precipitous decline of elephant herds, which had been poached mercilessly for their tusks.

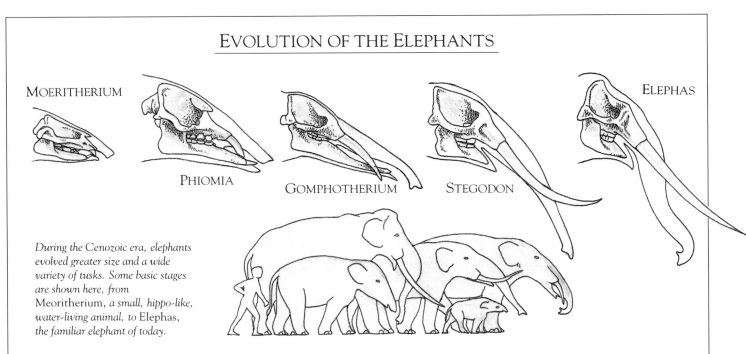

## EVOLUTION OF THE ELEPHANTS

MOERITHERIUM

PHIOMIA

GOMPHOTHERIUM

STEGODON

ELEPHAS

*During the Cenozoic era, elephants evolved greater size and a wide variety of tusks. Some basic stages are shown here, from Meoritherium, a small, hippo-like, water-living animal, to Elephas, the familiar elephant of today.*

humble beginnings of *Moeritherium*, and the skull and teeth took on the bizarre characteristics still seen in today's elephants. Although there were exceptions, the trend was toward a shorter jaw, fewer cheek teeth and steadily bigger incisor tusks. Many early elephants had not two, but four tusks, like *Gomphotherium* from the Miocene. Even odder was *Platybelodon*, in which the lower incisors were modified into shovels – a duck-billed elephant!

No doubt the most famous prehistoric elephants were the mammoths and mastodonts of the Pleistocene epoch. The common conception is of the "woolly mammoth" slogging through the frozen ice age wastes, but there were actually many different species, some indeed living in subarctic conditions, but others, like *Stegodon* of Asia, with its 13-foot/ 4-metre tusks, dwelling in bamboo forests.

The ice ages of the Pleistocene brought on some of the biggest elephants of all time, including *Mammuthus*

*trogontherii*, the giant steppe mammoth of Eurasia, more than 14 feet/4.2 metres high at the shoulder. Mastodonts and mammoths (differences in the teeth separate the two) often sported huge, curving tusks that swept up and back from the front of the face – not down and inward, as they were mounted on the first reconstructed fossils unearthed in the 19th century.

## PLATYBELEDON

Platybeledon *was a four-tusked mastodont, with short tusks (modified canine teeth) in the upper jaw and broad tusks (modified* incisor teeth) in the lower jaw. It is generally assumed that Platybeledon *used its shovel tusks to scrape up aquatic plants; the* short upper tusks may have helped to hold the food as the trunk pushed it into the mouth. The animal lived in Asia, Europe and Africa.

# PRIMATES AND THE GREAT APES

It is hard to be objective about the evolution of primates. This is not just another group of mammals that succeeded – this is about us. The primates, that "highest" of mammal orders, are also one of the oldest, having their origins as early as the end of the Cretaceous or beginning of the Paleocene epoch. These primitive primates, which may have arisen from arboreal insectivore stock, were similar to the lemurs of today, squirrel-like in shape but with the characteristic opposable thumb. Traditionally, primates were believed to have evolved in North America, but recent finds in China suggest that Asia may deserve the honour.

As the Paleocene epoch ran into the Eocene, the primate line split – one branch leading to the lemurs and bushbaby, the prosimians, the other branch giving rise to the anthropoids, as modern monkeys and apes are known. The first clear anthropoid we know of is *Amphipithecus*, found in Asian deposits about 45 million years old. The anthropoids split several more times – most notably in the Oligocene, when the ancestors of the New World monkeys first appeared, and in the Miocene, when the Old World monkeys and the ancestors of the apes parted ways.

**ABOVE: The world's smallest true monkey, the pygmy marmoset of the Amazon has a body which is just 5 inches/ 12 centimetres long. This tiny primate feeds by chewing small holes in tree trunks and lapping up the sap that runs out.**

## PRONCONSUL

*One of the most famous of the early apes, Proconsul is the centre of many arguments about the ancestry of humans. The first specimens, from the early Miocene, were found in Kenya. Since then, about eight species from its genus have been discovered around the Mediterranean and in East Africa. Until recently many scientists thought Proconsul was a direct ancestor of humans, but it is now seen as an ape, on the common line to modern apes and humans.*

The New World monkeys are arboreal, with long, prehensile tails in all but two species and universally flat, wide-spaced nostrils. The Old World monkeys, on the other hand, have closely spaced nostrils that point down (look in a mirror for a handy example), and many species are tailless; in addition, many have given up life in the trees and have become ground-dwelling animals.

The apes, which appeared in the middle Miocene, form three closely related groups – the gibbons and siamang of Asia; the orangutan; and the chimpanzee, gorilla and man. While the gorilla was long thought the closest ape to man, DNA studies have proved that the chimp is our nearest relative – so near, in fact, that in purely genetic terms chimps and humans are 98 per cent identical.

One of the most fascinating of the fossil primates was the largest ever – the huge ape *Gigantopithecus blacki*, which inhabited the bamboo forests of Southeast Asia during the Pleistocene. A second, smaller species, *G. giganteus* from India, lived during the Miocene.

**ABOVE: Primates split from the main mammalian stem rather early on, perhaps during the late Cretaceous period. This is a woolly monkey of the South American rain forest.**

**BELOW: Mostly bluff, a male lowland gorilla bares his fangs in a threat display that may lead to a ground-slapping, earth-shaking charge to frighten off a rival or threat.**

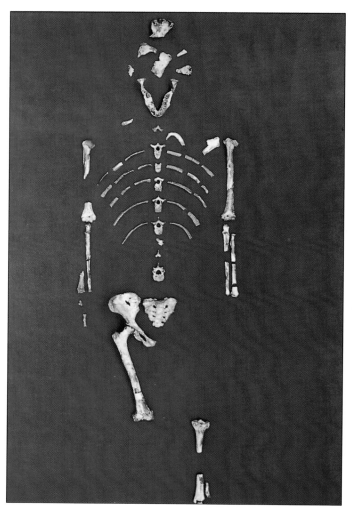

**ABOVE: The most famous image of a human fossil from the 1970s – "Lucy". She is the best specimen of *Australopithecus afarensis*, the oldest human, collected from Ethiopia. The remains show nearly half of the skeleton of a tiny adult, about 48 inches/ 1.2 metres tall. The skull shows that Lucy had relatively human brain-body proportions, and her legs, knees and feet were adapted for fully upright human walking. The bones are slightly more than 3 million years old.**

**ABOVE: Modern techniques of biochemical analysis have shown that chimpanzees are** human's closest relatives, sharing as much as 98 per cent of our genetic material.

G. blacki was an amazing creature; judging from the size of the jaws and teeth found so far (and using modern apes as a guide), it stood 10 feet/3 metres tall but probably walked on its knuckles, much as a modern chimp or gorilla. Microscopic examination of Gigantopithecus teeth have shown minuscule pieces of silica of the sort found in bamboo, as well as scratches in the tooth enamel caused by them. It seems very likely that this biggest of apes fed on bamboo, much as the giant panda that shared its habitat.

### HAIRY GIANTS

Recent excavations in Vietnam by joint United States-Vietnamese teams have proved that Gigantopithecus lived at the same time as Homo erectus, our direct ancestor. The scientists doing the digging have proposed the unusual theory that the encounters between the giant ape and H. erectus made such an impact on the early humans that they passed the story down through the generations. This, they think, could explain why almost every culture in the world has legends about giant, hairy apemen, like the sasquatch of North American and the yeti of Asia. Although maybe unlikely, the theory has some credibility.

# PICTURE CREDITS

Erwin & Peggy Bauer: 42, 43, 44, 56, 57 B, 65, 73 B, 76, 77, 80, 83, 91 B, 92. Richard Day: 37 T, 87. Darren Douglass: 15 B, 29. Michael H. Francis: 17 T, 90. Carl A. Hess: 19 T, 35, 37 B. Joe McDonald: 15 T, 21 B, 31 B, 46, 47 B, 60, 61, 68 T, 70 T&B, 71 T, 72, 78, 79 B, 81 L, 85, 91 T, 93 T, 96 BL, 97. Neal & Mary Jane Mishler: 71 B. Robert Montgomery: 86 T. Tom W. Parkin/Pathfinder: 33, 34 B, 89 T. Gregory K. Scott: 17 B, 67 L. Scott Weidensaul: 7 (5 pictures), 8 T, 9 T&B, 13 R, 20 R, 22, 23 T&B, 28 B, 30, 31 T, 36, 41 TL&TR, 48, 49, 50, 51 B&T, 63 T, 81 R, 86 B, 88 B, 89 B, 95 T, 96 T.

Danny McBride: gatefold artwork (including only first five animals). Graham Rosewarne: animal reconstructions (except as above). Jim Robins: skeletal diagrams. Elizabeth Sawyer: illustrations on page 11.